CW01022239

ARTIST DESIGNED TEXTILES 1940

ARTISTS' TEXTILE

Geoffrey Rayner
Richard Chamberlain
Annamarie Stapleton

Antique Collectors' Club

Geoff Rayner and Richard Chamberlain have run the Target Gallery in London's West End for fifteen years, specialising in design since 1945. The Gallery moved from its original location in 2006 and now functions from offices in London's Fitzroy Square. Geoff and Richard held a number of well-received exhibitions at the gallery, notably 'Design in Tandem: The Work Of Robin and Lucienne Day', 1999, and 'Reconstruction: Designers in Britain, 1945-51' in 2001. They also co-curated and co-authored, with Annamarie Stapleton, the exhibitions and accompanying books, 'Austerity to Affluence: British Art and Design 1945 -1962', and 'Artist's Textiles in Britain 1945-1970', held at the Fine Art Society London, in 1997 and 2003, respectively. In 2006 they co-curated with Annamarie the exhibition 'Alastair Morton 1910-1963', also held at the Fine Art Society. More recently, in 2009-10, they participated as advisors for the 'Design On Screen' award winning documentary film 'Contemporary Days: The Designs of Robin and Lucienne Day', directed by Murray Grigor, and also in 2009 they co-authored with Annamarie 'Jacqueline Groag, Textile & Pattern Design: Wiener Werkstätte to American Modern'. In 2011 they also co-curated and lent to several major exhibitions of Modern Design, 'Robin and Lucienne Day: Design and the Modern Interior' held at both at the Pallant House Gallery, Chichester and the PM Gallery, Ealing, and 'Terence Conran: The Way We Live Now' held at the Design Museum, London. In 2012 Geoff Rayner was guest curator of the 'Pop Design' exhibition at the Fashion and Textile Museum, Bermondsey, and he and Richard Chamberlain continue to work with clients from their base in Fitzroy Square.

Annamarie Stapleton is a specialist in nineteenth and twentieth century design and has been involved in a number of pioneering exhibitions at the Fine Art Society, London. Publications include 'John Moyr Smith: A Victorian Designer'; 'Austerity to Affluence: British Art & Design 1945-1962', 'Jacqueline Groag' and 'The Ambassador: Fashion and Trade in Post War Britain'. She has contributed articles to 'Country LIfe' and the 'Decorative Arts Society Journal' for which she is currently editor. Annamarie is a director of the Fine Art Society plc, British Rowing and the British Paralympic Association.

ARTIST DESIGNED TEXTILES 1940-1976

ARTISTS' TEXTILES

© 2012 Geoffrey Rayner, Richard Chamberlain, Annamarie Stapleton

World copyright reserved

ISBN 978-1-85149-629-7

The rights of Geoffrey Rayner, Richard Chamberlain and Annamarie Stapleton to be identified as authors of this work has been asserted by them in accordance with the Copyright, Designs and Patents Act 1988

All rights reserved. No part of this publication may be reproduced, stored in a retrieval system, or transmitted in any form or by any means electronic, mechanical, photocopying, recording or otherwise, without the prior permission of the publisher

Every effort has been made to secure permission to reproduce the images contained within this book, and we are grateful to the individuals and institutions who have assisted in this task. Any errors are entirely unintentional, and the details should be addressed to the publisher.

British Library Cataloguing-in-Publication Data

A catalogue record for this book is available from the British Library

Series designed and typeset by John and Orna Designs, London

Printed in China

Published in England by the Antique Collectors' Club Ltd., Woodbridge, Suffolk

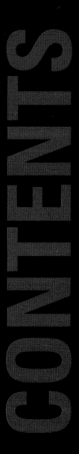

CONTENTS

Acknowledgements

Angela Brill; Catherine Britton; H.Kirk Brown III and Jill. A. Wiltse; Stephen Bruce and Serendipity 3, New York; Greg Burchard, Matt Wrbican and the Andy Warhol Museum, Pittsburgh; Anna Buruma & The Liberty Archive; Jane Bowen & Antoinette Rowling of the River and Rowing Museum, Henley; Christine Boydell; Trevor and Elaine Chamberlain; Geoffrey Clarke; Judith Collins; Anthony D'Offay; Mark Eastment; Michael Eftihiou; Lynn Felsher Nacmias and The Fashion Institute of Technology, New York; Hugh Fowler-Wright; Francesca Franchi and the archive of the Royal Opera House, Covent Garden; David Fraser Jenkins; Orna Frommer-Dawson; Francesca Galloway; Jennifer Harris and Frances Pritchard and the Whitworth Art Gallery; Gregory Herringshaw and the Cooper-Hewitt National Design Museum, New York; Lesley Jackson; Elsbeth Juda; Sue Kerry and the Warner Archive; David Kewn; Richard Morphet; Kitty Morris; Alison Morton; The National Archive of Art and Design; The National Art Library; Dennis Nothdruft and Alison McCann, the Fashion and Textile Museum, London; Linda Parry and Lucy Pratt and the Victoria & Albert Museum; Andrew McIntosh Patrick; John Rombola; Josephine Ross; The R.I.B.A Archive; James Smith; The Henry Moore Foundation; Jonathan Richards; Mary Schoeser; Shanna Shelby; Sir Paul Smith; Sheila Schwartz and The Saul Steinberg Foundation, New York; Steve Tanner; The Tate Library and Archive; Geoff Windram.

Every effort has been made to secure permission to reproduce the images contained within this book, and we are grateful to the individuals and institutions who have assisted in this task. Any errors or omissions are entirely unintentional, and the details should be addressed to the publisher.

ACKNOWLEDGEMENTS

"It is my personal opinion that fabric design rightfully belongs in the category of the Fine Arts, ... as an art, it is just as important as good architecture, and certainly is more closely associated with our everyday living than are paintings." Ruth Reeves, 1946.[1]

INTRODUCTION 1910–1939

Geoffrey Rayner

Introduction
1910-1939

The remarkable involvement of fine artists with the design of industrially produced textiles for the mass market after the Second World War was, essentially, a response to the fast-growing democratic franchise in technologically advanced, and increasingly sophisticated, industrial western societies, particularly in Britain and the United States of America. From the English artist and textile designer William Morris onwards, many artists in the late nineteenth and early twentieth centuries attempted to make their work relevant to the lives of ordinary people. Like Morris, they came to see the concept of design as an appropriate way to achieve this, but most of these early attempts by artists to engage with modern twentieth-century life foundered on negative and elitist cultural attitudes to new materials, inexpensive industrial manufacturing methods and mass marketing. Instead, they relied on expensive traditional handcrafts and exclusive retail outlets to produce and sell their textiles. Apart from a few exceptions, such as those in Russia, artist-designed textiles between the two World Wars were largely the prerogative of a wealthy minority. Morris's oft quoted exclamation of frustration and despair on realising the failure of his work to touch directly the lives of ordinary people, 'I have spent my life ministering to the swinish luxury of the rich'[2] would have been equally true for many others.

It was not until the 1940s, in the aftermath of the Second World War, that a more liberal and inclusive society emerged which encouraged a new social and cultural climate that enabled the work of artists, many of international fame, to be integrated directly, through the medium of textile design, in the daily lives of ordinary people. The architectural and design historian Nikolaus Pevsner, writing in 1946 in response to some of the first artist textiles to be produced in the post-war era, felt the chances of success for the involvement of artists in textile design were greater then, as:

1 Fashion textile, 'Charlot', designed by Raoul Dufy for Bianchini-Férier, Lyons, circa 1919, like the thousands of designs he produced for Bianchini over a sixteen-year period this is block-printed.

[1] Ruth Reeves, 'Design Creates Opportunities', *Craft Horizons*, May 1946, vol. 5 no. 13, p. 6.

[2] E.P. Thompson, lecture to the William Morris Society, 1959. First published in *Persons and Polemics, Historical Essays*, Merlin Press 1994, pp. 66-76.

An expression of anger and alienation that Morris made when supervising work on the house of the Northern ironmaster Sir Lowthian Bell in 1876, when he turned suddenly on his patron 'like a wild beast'.

[3] Nikolaus Pevsner, 'Can Painters Design Textiles?', *Art In Industry*, vol. 1, no. 1, Calcutta, December 1946, pp. 11-17.

[4] René Simon Lévy, 'The Fabrics of Raoul Dufy', essay first published in exhibition catalogue *Raoul Dufy*, eds. Bryan Robertson and Sarah Wilson, Arts Council of Great Britain, Hayward Gallery, London, 9 November 1983-5 February 1986, p. 106.

[5] Ibid. p. 99.

"Art in the past twenty or thirty years has moved away from narrow representational concerns. Problems of pure form and colour, that is of pattern, are now the chief content of art. Hence the stylised, sometimes elementary, sometimes barbaric look of a good deal of modern painting and sculpture."[3]

Pevsner is referring to the gallimaufry of avant-garde art movements that had arisen in the early decades of the twentieth century under the umbrella of 'Modernism'. The title of

Pevsner's article, 'Can Painters Design Textiles?', also raised the important issue of whether painters and sculptors could function within the applied arts without loss of artistic integrity and their work being reduced to the level of superficial ornamentation. Another problem of even greater pertinence for avant-garde artists in the early twentieth century was society's high regard for the unique autographic work of art compared to the low status generally given to the industrially manufactured mass-produced object. It was, in part, as a resolution of these concerns, especially those of the Fauvists, Futurists and Constructivists, that many artists became involved with textile design which, like graphic design and book illustration, had a natural correlation with print making and quickly came to be seen, particularly in mid-century Britain and America, as a legitimate and important aspect of an artist's work.

1911-1933. France: Paul Poiret, Raoul Dufy and Bianchini-Férier

The first successful groundbreaking involvement of a twentieth century artist with textile design was that of the Fauvist painter Raoul Dufy, whose initial commission to design textiles came from the great Parisian couturier Paul Poiret, for his interior decorating firm Maison Martine. At that time a strong interest in primitive art and folk-art and the naive charm and apparent innocence of children's art was widespread amongst artists of the avant-garde, and Poiret's offer was largely inspired by the archaic 'primitive' qualities of Dufy's woodcut illustrations for Guillaume Apollinaire's 'Le Bestiaire ou Cortège d'Orphée', 1910. Dufy's subsequent synthesis of the stylised designs and vigorous outlines of his woodcuts, with the surface simplification and pure colour of Fauvism, and the overlapping and juxtaposed planes of Cubism, resulted in a series of powerful and original textile designs, whose charming and scintillating *faux naïf* and spontaneity of expression chimed instantly with Poiret's aesthetic aims for the Maison Martine.

However, Dufy's and Poiret's collaboration was short lived, a victim of its own success, for in less than a year, in 1912, Dufy signed an exclusive contract with the important and long established Lyon-based textile manufacturer Bianchini-Férier. Dufy's contract with Bianchini was to last some sixteen years, during which time he created over 4000 designs.

Although the principal artistic influences on Dufy's designs were Fauvist and Cubist aesthetics, his awareness and appreciation of other developments in Modern art, such as Abstraction, Constructivism and Futurism, are apparent in his later abstract geometric designs for Bianchini, and the extraordinary Futurist design, 'Charlot', in which Charlie Chaplin's little tramp is depicted against a cityscape of skyscrapers linked by rolling ribbons of cinematic film. The speed and movement of the modern city are expressed in the kinetic colour wheels created by Charlie's twirling cane and the shooting rays of the electric street lights (Plate 1).

That textile design formed a major part of Dufy's *oeuvre* there can be no doubt, given the long and successful duration of his involvement in the industry – until, at least, 1933 – and the vast number of designs he produced in that time. For Dufy, his work in the applied arts was more than merely bread and butter and the relationship between his woodcut prints and block-printed textiles is extremely close. Indeed, he reworked many of his illustrations for Apollinaire's 'Bestiaire' as designs for a wide variety of woven or block-printed silk or linen textiles, the latter being used for his well-known 'Toiles de Tournon' range for Bianchini.

Dufy's printed textiles are original artistic creations. At first he carved his own wood blocks, although later in the Bianchini period they were produced by a firm named Dournel, 'who took great care to respect the "rustic" irregularities of Dufy's originals.'[4] It is made clear by René Simon Lévy that Dufy saw his prints as of equal validity, whatever medium they were produced in:

"The technique of printing on cloth is exactly the same as for printing on paper, and Dufy was very familiar with it. Some blocks (for no rollers were ever used there) were used in fact on both cloth and paper, and some of these prints still exist: I found in the Bianchini-Férier collection a charming vignette on paper which was also printed all over a piece of satin belonging to Mme Poiret."[5]

Dufy's remarkable achievements in the field of textile design had a widespread influence on the work of artists internationally. This was particularly so in Britain where a nascent avant-garde were just becoming aware of French Modern art under the enthusiastic guidance of the academic and art critic and painter, Roger Fry. He initially achieved this by organising and curating two seminally important exhibitions of contemporary French painting in 1910 and 1912, for which he coined the term 'post-Impressionism'. The second of these was especially influential, as a large number of Fauvist and Cubist works were shown, many by Matisse and Picasso. Amongst the disparate groups of artists that attempted to coalesce around this window onto European Modernism were Fry's close associates: the 'Bloomsbury' painters, Vanessa Bell and Duncan Grant, and, though soon to break away to form the Vorticist movement, the painters Wyndham Lewis, Frederick Etchells, William Roberts, Edward Wadsworth and the French sculptor Henri Gaudier-Brzeska.

Although the members of this short-lived coterie exhibited jointly as the Grafton Group, they are better known today under the umbrella of the Omega Workshops, an artists' cooperative for the decorative arts, set up by Fry ostensibly to provide a reliable source of income for those involved. Fry, however, had another more ambitious agenda for the workshops, part of which was to expose and break down what he saw as 'the erroneous distinction between fine and applied art'.[6]

Fry's concerns were shared by many avant-garde artists, architects and designers in the late nineteenth and early twentieth centuries: their ultimate goal being the achievement of the total work of art through the unity of a building's design with that of its interiors and furnishings in a complete integration of art, architecture and design; what Josef Hoffmann and the Secessionists referred to as the 'Gesamtkunstwerk'. This could be accomplished through the work of a single architect, such as Charles Rennie Mackintosh, working in tandem with his wife Margaret Macdonald, or as a collaboration between a group of architects, designers and artists, the supreme example of which is probably the Palais Stoclet in Brussels: the work of the Wiener Werkstätte. It was not until the building of the Palais in 1905 that the integration of the work of artists within such a collaboration was successfully achieved, the greatest example being the painter Gustav Klimt's magnificent mosaic frieze for the dining room.

Under Hoffmann's inspired leadership many artists of the Vienna Secession, even those as radical as Oskar Kokoschka and Egon Schiele, were able to create uncompromised designs for the Wiener Werkstätte. The influence of the Werkstätte was wide, particularly in Germany where a similarly decorative style known as 'L'Art Munichois' had been developed in Munich, which, like the Werkstätte, drew on both naive and folk-art, and also that of children, as sources of fresh and spontaneous inspiration.

Pattern design, particularly that of textiles, became an increasingly important aspect of both the Werkstätte's output and 'L'Art Munichois' and Paul Poiret's admiration for their decorative styles, which he shared with Raoul Dufy, was influential in his decision to set up a studio for the decorative arts, the École Martine, in 1911: the same year in which Dufy created his first textiles for Poiret. That the Martine provided something of a model for the Omega Workshops is made clear by Roger Fry in a letter of December 1912 where, referring to the potential of the 'decorative methods' of post-Impressionism, he writes:

"Already in France Poiret's École Martine shows what delightful possibilities are revealed in this direction … My workshop would be carried on on similar lines and might probably work in conjunction with the École Martine by mutual exchange of ideas and products."[7]

Fry would already have been acquainted with the work of Poiret's atelier and Dufy's textiles for, in November 1911, the restaurateur Marcel Boulestin had opened a shop in London: "which sold the whole Martine range, including Dufy's work … The silks, the velvets, the linens, the knick-knacks and the wallpapers came from the Martine."[8]

That textile design was seen at the Omega as an entirely appropriate medium

2 **Opposite** 'Cypren', block-printed silk chiffon scarf, designed by Josef Hoffmann for the Wiener Werkstätte, circa 1910.

3 **Left** Textile swatches by the Omega Workshops, 1913, these block-printed linens are attributed to Roger Fry, Vanessa Bell, Duncan Grant & Frederick Etchells.

[6] Judith Collins, *The Omega Workshops*, Secker & Warburg, London 1983, p. 4.

[7] Roger Fry, letter to George Bernard Shaw, 11 December 1912: add. MS SO534, British Library.

[8] Sarah Wilson, 'Raoul Dufy: Tradition, Innovation, Decoration, 1900-1925', *Raoul Dufy*, eds. Robertson and Wilson, 1986, p. 74.

for artistic expression is immediately apparent in the series of printed linen and jacquard woven furnishing textiles, carpets and rugs and embroideries which formed a considerable part of the workshops' output and are amongst some of their most successful products. The majority of the Omega textiles are the work of Fry himself, Vanessa Bell and Duncan Grant, although Frederick Etchells was probably responsible for one of the printed range and the design of an extraordinary carpet. It is, however, the printed textiles of 1913 which are remarkable for the purely abstract language of their designs which relate, although a year earlier, to Bell and Grant's brief but important foray into abstract painting which, in Grant's case, has been described as:

"An extreme moment in European abstraction in which ... by eschewing any mimetic reference, he has taken his work into a realm of speculative abstraction unprecedented at that time."[9]

The artists' textiles of the Omega Workshops, the first in Britain, are probably one of their most significant achievements, the influence of which continued to be felt in Britain well into the 1950s (Plate 3).

The avant-garde art scene in London between the two World Wars owed much to the brief but lively encounter with European Modernism afforded by the activities of the Omega Workshops and the Vorticist movement. The Vorticists had strong links with Italian Futurism and were totally engaged with the concept of 'Modernity'. Like the Futurist Giacomo Balla they were also concerned with the arbitrary distinction between fine and applied art and the breaking down of disciplinary boundaries. In 1914 members of the group, under the leadership of Wyndham Lewis, had set up a workshop for the applied arts – the short-lived Rebel Art Centre.

Their most influential foray into design was the publication of two issues of the magazine *Blast*, which the Russian Constructivist El Lissitsky saw as a precursor of the revolution in graphic design that occurred in Russia and Germany in the 1920s[10]. Almost everybody who was later anybody in Modern British art between the two World Wars was caught up in the vicious cross-currents occurring in the acrimonious debate betwixt opposing poles of the Omega Workshops and the Vorticists. However, by 1919 the energy and motivation generated between these had been exhausted and the London avant-garde played out. The mood of many British artists in the aftermath of the cataclysm of the First World War was elegiac and any interaction with the applied arts was at a low ebb.

4a and 4b Embroidered and block-printed silk robe designed by Wyndham Lewis, circa 1914, either for the Rebel Art Centre or the Omega Workshops.

* This hand-blocked art silk robe was assessed by Dr Linda Parry of the Victoria and Albert Museum's Department of Textiles to be the work of an avant-garde English artist, c1914. It was subsequently seen by the authority on the Omega Workshops and the Rebel Art centre, Dr Judith Collins, formerly of the Tate Gallery, London. who identified it as the work of the Vorticist artist Wyndham Lewis. Although closely related to Lewis's slightly earlier applied designs for the Omega Workshops and the Cabaret Theatre Club / the Cave of the Golden Calf, Dr Collins considers this robe to date from 1914 and the period of Lewis's involvement with the Rebel Art Centre.

[9] Richard Shone, *The Art of Bloomsbury*, Tate Gallery Publishing Ltd, London 1999, p. 155.

[10] Richard Weston, *Modernism*, Phaidon Press Ltd, London 1996, p.89.

Amongst the artists briefly associated with the Omega Workshops, and who subsequently counted textile design as part of their work, was the painter Paul Nash. Another was Nash's former fellow student at the Slade School of Art, the painter, designer and craft-worker Phyllis Barron. She, with her partner Dorothy Larcher and their former apprentice Enid Marx, played a pivotal role in the 1920s revival of hand block-printed textiles as a craft activity. The production facilities of these craft workshops were, however, limited and, for example, Elspeth Little, proprietor of the London based gallery Modern Textiles, was obliged to use the professional services of G P & J Baker when she received an order for thirty yards of fabric from the interior decorator Syrie Maugham. The textiles of these craft-workers were expensive and exclusive luxury products, created for a small, wealthy minority, which, despite the superficially smart modernity of their designs, were 'ideologically much more in tune with the Arts and Crafts tradition'.[11]

A project decidedly more in sync with European developments in artist designed textiles was Cryséde, set up in 1923 by Alec Walker for the high quality production of art inspired block-printed silk for the fashion market. Walker, a member of an old established family of Yorkshire silk weavers, had founded Cryséde in the Cornish town of Newlyn following his marriage to a member of the town's thriving artists' colony.

Amongst Walker's many artist friends living in Newlyn at that time were the sculptor Frank Dobson and the painters Ernest and Dod Proctor and Cedric Morris. It was Ernest Proctor who first encouraged Walker to develop his painting abilities and was later instrumental in bringing about his meeting with Raoul Dufy. Walker visited Paris in 1923 to buy or commission designs for Cryséde, but found the best French artists impossible to get hold of and the cost of their designs prohibitive.

While in Paris, Walker was introduced to Dufy through a mutual friend of the Proctors, but Dufy's exclusive contract to Bianchini-Férier did not allow him to help. However, impressed by the charm of the naivety and strong colours of Walker's untutored paintings, he encouraged him to create his own designs. Following Dufy's

5 Above 'Penberth Farm', block-printed silk dress fabric, designed by Alec Walker for Cryséde Ltd, circa 1925.

6 Opposite Dress, circa 1930, made from block-printed linen, designed by Alec Walker for Cryséde Ltd. This design was originally block-printed on silk in 1925, and on linen from 1928/9.

[11] Hazel Clark, Phyllis Barron and Dorothy Larcher, *Contemporary Designers*, ed. Anne Lee Morgan, Macmillan Publishers Ltd, London 1984, p. 46.

[12] Hazel Berriman, *Cryséde, The Unique Textile Designs of Alec Walker*, Royal Institution of Cornwall, Royal Cornwall Museum, Truro, 1993, p. 19; quote from Frank Rutter, *The Studio*, 1928.

[13] Patrick Heron, 'Tom Heron: a biographical note', *The Decorative Arts Society 1850 to the Present Journal*, No. 4, p. 34.

advice Walker subsequently produced a remarkable series of Fauvist influenced textiles, all translations of his paintings (Plate 5). Cryséde silks were both an artistic and commercial triumph. The art critic Frank Rutter, writing in *The Studio*, described them as having 'a unity and distinction which gave them a unique decorative value in sympathy with Modernist aims.'[12]

This runaway success necessitated a rapid expansion of the business, for which Walker enlisted the help of a friend from his Yorkshire days: Tom Heron, father of the painter Patrick Heron. Walker and Heron's personal compatibility and mutual interest in art resulted in so successful a joint management team that, by 1926, the firm had over 7000 mail order customers and it was soon necessary to relocate Cryséde's print works to much larger premises in St Ives. By the early thirties the company had a chain of twenty-two retail shops, but, in part unhappy and stressed by the rapidity of the company's expansion, Walker suffered a temporary breakdown in 1929 and he and Heron parted company in 1933.

Tom Heron then set up a new company on similar lines to Cryséde: Cresta Silks, in Welwyn Garden City, Hertfordshire. His brief for Cresta was, more or less, that of Walker's for Cryséde: the production of artist-designed, block printed fashion silks. Many were designed by Walker's old friend from Newlyn, Cedric Morris and Paul Nash who, as well as providing new designs, transferred the production of earlier ones to Cresta. Heron's son, Patrick, also designed fashion yardage and scarves for the company both before and after the Second World War. Cryséde and Cresta were both remarkable and commercially successful experiments using Fauvist ideas within the medium of textile design (Plate 6). Alec Walker creating what Patrick Heron has described as, 'brilliant designs of great originality.'[13]

Whilst on a second visit to Paris in 1924, Alec Walker was introduced – most probably by Raoul Dufy – to the American painter Ruth Reeves, arguably the most significant American textile designer of the twentieth century. Having first studied at the California School of Design in San Francisco and the Pratt Institute in Brooklyn, Reeves was awarded a scholarship in 1913 to the progressive Art Students League in New York. After completing her studies there she worked for a time as a batik artist, and in 1916 won a prize in the first textile design competition organized by *Women's Wear Daily* magazine, where she also worked in various capacities until 1921. That year she left the United States for Paris, to study painting at the Académie Moderne as a student of Fernand Léger. She also appears to have had some contact with Dufy, which her introduction to Alec Walker seems to confirm. That a degree of friendship subsequently developed between Walker and Reeves is clearly indicated by the watercolour portrait he made of her in the sketchbook he used during the visit.[14]

Dufy's influence on Reeves's work is at its strongest in her ground-breaking collection of textiles and wall hangings commissioned, after her return from Paris in 1928, by the New York-based textile manufacturer, W & J Sloane, for their display in the 'Decorative Metalwork and Cotton Textiles' section of the 'Third International Exhibition of Contemporary Industrial Art', held at New York's Metropolitan Museum of Art in 1930. Amongst these were the printed cotton textiles 'Manhattan' and 'American Scene', both of which owe a stylistic debt to Dufy's 'Toiles de Tournon', which depict scenes of modern French life in a similar manner. In the exhibition's catalogue, 'Manhattan', with its design of vignettes of everyday life enveloped and dwarfed by the skyscrapers and landmarks of New York City, is somewhat equivocally entitled 'Canyons of Steel'.[15] It is the quintessential twentieth century textile (Plate 7).

Subsequently Reeves rarely accepted commissions or designed for commercial production, preferring to print her textiles in her studio. There are, however, several remarkable exceptions the most celebrated being her textile and carpet designs, commissioned by the industrial and interior designer Donald Deskey, for the interiors of the newly built Radio City Music Hall, which opened in New York in 1932. In 1933 she conceived her Hudson River series of textiles, for which she was awarded a fellowship grant from the Gardner School Alumni

Foundation, which subsidised the work of distinguished women. The Fellowship's chairperson explained,

'It was felt that her [Reeves] idea of perpetrating the present Hudson River scene in fabrics might initiate as significant a trend as that which produced the fascinating old French Toiles which recorded in that medium the story of French life of that day'. Once more there is an echo of Dufy's 'Toiles de Tournon'.[16]

When, in 1934, Reeves turned from Europe to the Americas in her quest for inspiration, she received a Carnegie Travelling Fellowship to study traditional textiles in Guatemala. On her return to New York in 1935, an exhibition was held of her influential Guatemalan inspired textile designs, which she termed 'Adaptations' (Plate 8). The introduction to the exhibition catalogue was written by M D C Crawford, a one-time editor of *Women's Wear Daily*, whom Reeves had previously helped with his classic work, *The Heritage of Cotton*, 1924, a highly influential book, greatly admired by Alec Walker, from which he gained many sympathetic ideas.[17] Five of Reeve's designs, derived from traditional Guatemalan patterns, were also produced commercially and retailed, in 1935, by the well-known store R H Macy & Co. (Plate 9).

Although she continued to design and produce textiles, Reeves's subsequent career became increasingly academic, with a greater emphasis on research and teaching. Her ongoing researches into, and visual recording of, the pattern making traditions of the Americas, both colonial and indigenous, were notably supported by the scholar Holger Cahill, director of the Federal Art Project, the cultural branch of Franklin D Roosevelt's New Deal Program, the Work Projects Administration (WPA). Her researches were further facilitated, in 1940, by a Guggenheim Fellowship and later, in 1955, when she was given a Fulbright Fellowship to study in India. Following this she was appointed Advisor in Handicrafts to the Register General of India, for whom she documented craft traditions. Her greatest academic legacy is the Index of American Design, to which she was appointed national coordinator in 1936. To this day it remains an invaluable visual source of American cultural identity for artists, designers and academics.

Ruth Reeves's path as a textile designer eventually led her away from

7 Opposite 'Manhattan', a block-printed cotton, furnishing textile, designed by Ruth Reeves and produced by W & J Sloane. This design was exhibited at the International Exhibition of Metalwork & Cotton Textiles, 1930, under the title 'Canyons of Steel.'

8 Right This tablemat, designed and printed by Ruth Reeves, circa 1935, illustrates very well her interpretation of Guatemalan textiles in a thoroughly modern way. Reeves wrote of her work, 'Regardless of its original inspiration, it is firmly rooted within the framework of twentieth century design and ways of life.'

[14] Berriman, 1993, p. 18.

[15] *Catalogue of Decorative Metalwork and Cotton Textiles, the 3rd International Exhibition of Contemporary Industrial Art*, American Federation of Arts 1930-1931.

[16] Katie Rudolph, 'Overlooking Kingston' published on Helen Louise Allen Textile Collection website, www.textilecollection.wisc.edu

[17] Berriman, 1993, p. 18.

9 Detail of 'Guatemalan Document', designed and printed by Ruth Reeves circa 1935, and adapted here for a tablecloth. This design was one of a number Reeves titled 'Adaptations', which were exhibited in New York following her studies in Guatemala in 1934. A highly influential design, it was also used on an apparel weight fabric for a belted dress, and printed on heavy linen for curtains and upholstery.

Europe as a source of inspiration, but, possibly as a result of the success of her Dufy influenced textiles such as 'Manhattan', between 1930 and 1933, the American textile manufacturer, the Onondaga Silk Company, commissioned Raoul Dufy to design a series of fashion textiles. This project, Dufy's last recorded work in association with a commercial company, was thought at the time markedly unsuccessful, mainly because of the problems of coordination created by the distances involved, which resulted in what were considered dull and disappointing end products.[18]

Soon after the First World War, a number of American textile manufacturers sought to shake off the dominance of European, particularly French, design and to develop a more distinctly American modern style. The United States did not officially take part in the French design extravaganza of 1925, the Exposition Internationale des Arts Décoratifs et Industriels Modernes, and, in what seems almost a riposte, one American textile company, the Stehli Silks Corporation, launched the first of a remarkable range of silk dress fabrics, the 'Americana Prints' later that year.[19] Issued between 1925 and 1927, the range was an uncompromising series of sharp and witty, up to the minute designs by an eclectic mix of American artists, designers, cartoonists and celebrities. The most extraordinary is the group of designs derived from photographic images of everyday objects, such as sugar cubes and mothballs, by the distinguished photographer and painter Edward Steichen, which are prescient of 1960s Pop Art (Plate 10). Photographs by Steichen, and other well-known photographers, were also used in the later 1930s by the textile manufacturer Mallinson Fabrics, for a series of textiles called 'Camera Prints'.

10 'Mothballs and Sugarlumps', a printed silk designed by the photographer Edward Steichen for Stehli Silks Corporation, 1927. One of ten designs by Steichen for the firms groundbreaking 'Americana' series, described by Kneeland Green, the Art Director of Stehli, as 'silk designs that tell a story', for customers who were 'sick and tired of the conventional florals and polka dots.'

Although Fauvism had provided a starting point for the involvement of artists with textiles, by the 1920s the work of the Franco-Russian painter Sonia Delaunay-Terk, and that of her compatriots, the Constructivists Liubov Popova and Varvara Stepanova, had became increasingly influential. All three women came to textile design, although from different points of departure, through their commitment to one or another of the new art movements concerned with abstraction.

Delaunay's interest was originally inspired by the work of her husband Robert Delaunay, a form of pure abstract painting based on Robert's new theories of rhythmical and optical laws derived from the effects of simultaneous colour contrasts, which the poet Apollinaire had termed 'Orphism'. It was the kinetic qualities of these visual rhythms created by contrasting blocks of colour that led Delaunay to design textiles. In 1913 she created clothes for herself and Robert with abstract patterns of contrasting swirling colours, inspired by the rapid movements of dancers she had seen at a Parisian dance hall, the Bal Bullier. She had already created similar abstract designs in cloth for book covers and a bedspread for her son. While living in Spain during and shortly after the First World War, she had continued to design textiles and clothes which were sold in a shop she had opened in Madrid.

Delaunay did not differentiate between the artistic merit of her paintings and her textile and fashion designs and, from shortly after her return to Paris in 1920 until the mid-1930s, textiles formed the principal focus of her work. The kinetic visual effect of her textiles and clothing working in unity with the movement of the human body was for her a total art form. Her success reached its peak in 1925 when she was invited, with the couturier Jacques Heim, to create a 'simultaneous boutique' for the Paris Exposition Internationale des Arts Décoratifs et Industriels Modernes (Plate 11).

Although Delaunay's fellow country-women, Popova and Stepanova, came to similar conclusions and solutions, theirs was a very different perspective. Whereas Delaunay considered textile design an important aspect of her artistic *oeuvre* and her clientele were

11 Actor in a still from the film 'Le p'tit Parigot', wearing a dressing gown in a fabric designed by Sonia Delaunay, 1926.

[18] René Simon Lévy, 1983.

[19] Virginia Gardner Troy, *The Modernist Textile, Europe And America 1890-1940.* Lund Humphries, Aldershot, 2006, p. 109.

23

drawn from a wealthy international elite, these two Constructivists, working within a revolutionary socialist state, viewed the fine arts as activities of privilege and prestige, irrelevant in the modern world. Constructivist artists, like themselves, were concerned with real materials in real space and saw their role as 'Productivists' – responsible for designing well thought out, functional and utilitarian goods, which would come to replace sculpture and painting as cultural productions that could be effortlessly integrated into the daily lives of the proletariat.

Popova and Stepanova, like Delaunay, saw the design of a textile as integral to the clothing for which it was intended and created extraordinary designs for workers' clothing and sportswear in which the pattern design and the clothing's form and cut were conceived as a unity (Plates 13 and 14).

They worked for the First State Printed Calico Factory, Moscow, designing bold, abstract, geometric prints of careful proportions and subtle rhythms, many of which anticipated the hard-edged abstraction and Op Art of the 1950s and 1960s.

Liubov Popova died in 1924, at the age of 35. It has been written that she 'interpreted the human body as a kinetic construction emphasising its mobility in her light, efficient and democratic textile and dress design of 1923 and 1924.'[20] The same can equally be said of Delaunay and Stepanova.

Varvara Stepanova's textiles made a significant impact in the West when they were shown in the Soviet Pavilion at the 1925 Paris Exposition. But she and her husband, the Constructivist, Aleksandr Rodchenko – who had also designed textiles – soon after became completely involved with typography and graphic design, particularly of books, for the remainder of their working lives.

Another member of the Russian avant-garde, for whom textile design became an important part of his work, was Paul Mansouroff (Pavel Andreevitch Mansurov). He had been head of the experimental department of the Petrograd branch of the State Institute of Painterly Culture, Ginkhuk, which included amongst its teaching staff Kasimir Malevich, Mikhail Matiushin and Pavel Filonov, and all his life he remained one of the most consistent practitioners of abstract painting.

After leaving Russia in 1928, Mansouroff arrived in Paris, via Italy, as a penniless émigré in June 1929. Armed with letters of introduction from Vladimir Tatlin and Vladimir Mayakovsky, he was taken in by Sonia and Robert Delaunay and, through them, introduced to Picasso who,

12 Opposite Block-printed silk scarf designed by Sonia Delaunay, circa 1928. Delaunay's impressive body of work in textile design focused mainly on printed silks and linens for fashion, her work had something of a renaissance in her later career with companies such as Ascher and Liberty of London.

13 Right top Textile design and dresses made from the same fabric by Liubov Popova, circa 1923.

14 Right bottom Sports outfits designed by Vavara Stepanova, circa 1923.

[20] John E. Bowlt and Nicoletta Misler, *The Thyssen-Bornemisza Collection, Twentieth-Century Russian and East European Painting*, Zwemmer, Philip Wilson Publishers, London 1993, p. 19.

РАБОТЫ СТЕПАНОВОЙ

although admiring Mansouroff's work, was unsuccessful in obtaining an exhibition for him. Picasso told him, 'even if you are the Raphael of abstract art your painting will be of little interest to anyone.'[21]

At Sonia Delaunay's suggestion he took up textile design and through her received introductions to leading French textile manufacturers such as Bianchini-Férier. His career as a textile designer in the 1930s was extremely successful. He realised many projects for the great Parisian couture houses, Patou, Chanel, Lanvin and Schiaparelli amongst them. A tie silk designed by him for Maison Sulka (Plate 15) was worn by King Edward VIII at his marriage to Mrs Simpson[22] and carpets and textiles were commissioned from him for an exhibition of artists' textiles held in 1936 by Metz & Co. in Amsterdam. Later in the thirties the Irish and Scottish textile manufacturers, The Old Bleach Linen Company and Edinburgh Weavers, produced textiles to designs commissioned from him, giving these leading manufacturers the opportunity of a direct encounter with a member of the European avant-garde (Plate 16).

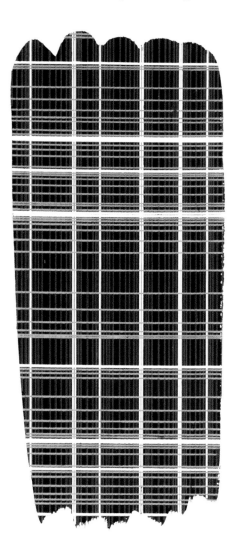

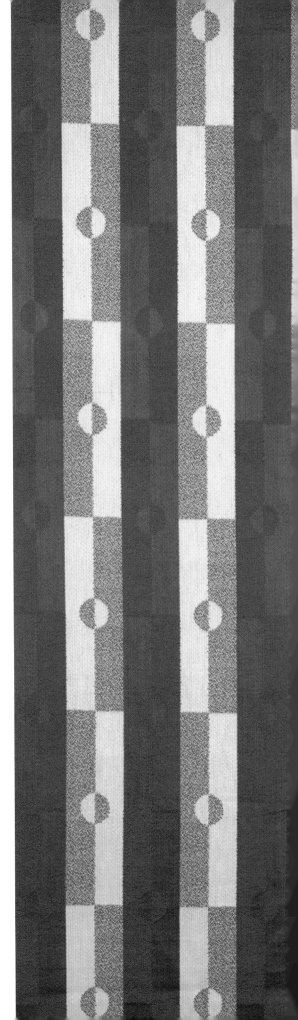

15 Right Tie silk designed by Paul Mansouroff for Maison Sulka, 1936. This is one of three variations for tie silks manufactured by Bianchini-Férier for Sulka, one of which was worn by King Edward VIII, Duke of Windsor, for his marriage to Mrs Simpson, 1937.

16 Far right Paul Mansouroff (attrib) for Edinburgh Weavers Ltd, jacquard woven cotton and linen textile of 'Constructivist' design, circa 1938.

[21] Exhibition catalogue, *Paul Mansouroff et l'avant-garde Russe*, Petrograd, Musée d'Art Moderne et d'Art Contemporain de la Ville de Nice, 1995, p. 194.

[22] Ibid. p. 145.

Inspired by developments in textile design elsewhere, the painter Allan Walton and his brother Roger set up Allan Walton Textiles in 1931: a spin-off of their family company, the cotton manufacturer John Walton of Collyhurst Ltd. Throughout the 1930s Walton pursued a policy of enlightened patronage, commissioning designs from painters and sculptors whom he encouraged to work free from the constraints of any commercial consideration or external influence. Among the resulting distinguished body of work produced by the disparate group of artists associated with Walton, are the Fauvist-inspired designs of Vanessa Bell and Duncan Grant, (Plate 17) and those less easily categorised by the sculptor Frank Dobson, a former member of Wyndham Lewis's short-lived extension of the Vorticist movement: Group X. This medley was further enriched by the self-consciously naive work of the painter Cedric Morris, and examples of geometric cubist-influenced abstraction and Constructivist designs by H J Bull and Thomas Bradley. The wide variety of art movements represented in Walton's project drew together the various threads of the avant-garde to give an overview of the contemporary growth of textile design as a medium of artistic expression.

Walton also played an important part in the development of artists' textiles through his experimental use of the comparatively new process of silk screen printing. Originally developed in Europe and the USA in the late nineteenth and early twentieth centuries from a form of Japanese printing using stencils, silk-screening had the advantage for the textile manufacturer of being a much quicker process than block-printing and was far more economically viable for short print runs than roller printing. From the artist's point of view the process greatly increased the freedom of the designer in its ability to reproduce both the spontaneity of a design and the fluidity and subtle nuances of brushwork and colour. The development of silk screen printing in the 1930s by companies like Allan Walton Textiles was of major significance for the future success of artist-designed textiles in the post-war era.

By the late 1930s other British textile manufacturers were commissioning designs from painters, The Old Bleach Linen Company for example commissioned Paul Nash, but, by far the most eminent of these manufacturers – and for the future development of artist-designed textiles the most significant – was

Edinburgh Weavers. James Morton, a member of the Morton textile dynasty and founder of Morton Sundour, set up Edinburgh Weavers in 1928 as a research unit to explore the creation, development and production of Modern textiles suitable for use in contemporary architectural settings, in tandem with Modern art and design. The running of Edinburgh Weavers was taken over in 1932 by James's son, the Constructivist painter, designer and weaver, Alastair Morton, who was responsible for the company's remarkable achievements in the field of artist-designed textiles, over the following thirty or so years.

The successful translation of an artist's work as a textile, particularly through the medium of weaving, was central to Morton's agenda. Ashley Havinden, a painter and leading graphic designer, remembered being told by Morton that it was his – Morton's – job, together with his assistants, to find a way of interpreting Havinden's designs in the weaving.[23] Havinden's textiles, alongside those of Ben Nicholson and Barbara Hepworth, were unveiled in 1937 when the company launched their celebrated range of 'Constructivist Fabrics'. The highly sensitive and subtle realisation of these artists' designs was a testament to Morton's painterly insight, craft skills and dedication to the task. In acknowledgement of the importance of Morton's contribution, Ben Nicholson wrote, in 1978, that:

"The designs made for Edinburgh Weavers were entirely brought about by him and I thought, and said that I felt they should have been (if he wished) attributed half to him and half to me."[24]

Nicholson and Hepworth had already experimented with textile design in the early 1930s and Nicholson with the design of rugs. In the post-war period they continued their interest in this field through their work with Zika and Lida Ascher (Plates 18 and 19).

Although the international production of artist-designed textiles between the two World Wars came to a temporary halt in 1939, their impact continued to reverberate well into the post-war era. By the early 1930s the involvement of leading artists in Europe with textile design, particularly in France, Russia and Austria, had already begun to falter in the face of increasing political crisis, economic depression and the all pervading influence of the anti-decorative stance of the International Modern Movement. It was in Britain, with the likes of Allan Walton

Textiles and Edinburgh Weavers, and in America, through the commitment and example of artists such as Ruth Reeves, coupled with the legacy of the involvement of the arts in the lives of ordinary people through the Federal Art Project and the WPA, that 'Painting By The Yard'[25] became such a remarkable success in the 1940s and 1950s.

In 1938, in reference to the achievement of artists then working with textiles, Ashley Havinden wrote:

"[they are] at their best a visual equivalent in terms of draped materials of the modern paintings and architecture of today."[26]

17 Opposite Screen-printed velvet furnishing textile, designed by Duncan Grant and intended for use on the P & O liner 'Queen Mary', produced by Allan Walton, 1936.

18 Top Ben Nicholson's 'Princess,' hand block-printed cotton, designed circa 1933.

19 Bottom "Slinky", a hooked wool rug designed by Ben Nicholson and worked by Joan Bravington, 1933.

[23] Richard Calvocoressi, 'Ashley's Textiles', *The Decorative Arts Society 1850 to the Present Journal*, no. 3, p. 7; quote from Ashley Havinden.

[24] Richard Calvocoressi, *Alastair Morton & Edinburgh Weavers, Abstract Art & Textile Design, 1935-46*, Scottish National Gallery of Modern Art, 29 April-29 May 1978, p. 11. Letter from Ben Nicholson to Calvocoressi dated 18 February 1978.

[25] Dilys Blum, title of her essay on artist designed textiles, 'Painting by the Yard', 2002.

[26] Richard Calvocoressi, 'Ashley's Textiles', *The Decorative Arts Society 1850 to the Present Journal* no. 3, p. 13; quote from Ashley Havinden.

In the mid-1940s two textile companies, Ascher Ltd. in Britain, and Wesley Simpson Custom Fabrics Inc. in the United States, more or less simultaneously launched remarkable collections of fashion fabrics and headsquares, with designs commissioned from internationally renowned painters and sculptors, initiating an unprecedented involvement of fine artists with the design of industrially produced textiles for the mass market.

THE 1940S

Britain:
Ascher Ltd:
Henri Matisse and
Henry Moore;
Horrockses
Fashions Ltd:
Graham
Sutherland and
Alastair Morton

During the 1920s and 1930s the concept of textile design as a legitimate part of an artist's work had grown steadily in Britain and, although hampered by the difficulties of the Second World War, the involvement of British artists with textile design remained a priority for parts of the industry. This was particularly so for the newly established Cotton Board's Centre for Colour, Design and Style in Manchester, whose director, James Cleveland Belle, had organised 'Design for Textiles by Fine Artists' in 1941; the first of many influential Cotton Board exhibitions held throughout the war. Amongst the artists who took part were the sculptor Frank Dobson and the painters Duncan Grant, Paul Nash, Graham Sutherland and John Piper. The exhibition was favourably reviewed in British *Vogue* under the title 'Palette and Loom'. Members of *Vogue*'s staff had 'guided and advised' the exhibition's organisers, and the reviewer was certain 'the results will be worthy of transatlantic interest'.[1] Another reviewer wrote:

"Almost every first rate artist and designer contributed to the exhibition, leading manufacturers have shown an active interest and outstanding designs were bought right away; ... to us there seems to be no doubt that valuable export orders will eventually follow."[2]

The Cotton Board's interest in artist-designed textiles at this time was largely due to the necessity of sustaining the vital export trade during wartime. Alan Walton, a leading pre-war manufacturer of artist-designed textiles, wrote in 1942 that:

"War conditions have severely limited production but the desirability of developing American interest in British textiles has been emphasised by the government, and manufacturers are trying to produce as much as possible for Export."[3]

1 Right Cover of the Ascher catalogue *The First Exhibition of Artist Designed Squares*, Lefevre Gallery, 1947.

2 Opposite Lucian Freud's winning design for furnishing fabric, shown at the East Anglian School of Painting and Drawing and published in *Art & Industry*, October 1942.

[1] Anon, 'Palette and Loom British Designs for British Fabrics', *Vogue*, London, June 1941, pp. 46-47.

[2] Anon, 'Creative Skill will Promote Sales', in *International Textiles*, 1941.

[3] Alan Walton, 'The Search for Design', in *Art & Industry*, October 1942, pp. 18-21.

The subject of Walton's article was a competition for textile design he had recently organised at the East Anglian School of Art; the school's Principal, the painter Cedric Morris, had previously designed textiles for Walton's company in the early 1930s. The student winner of the competition was the young painter Lucian Freud.

Although some British textile manufacturers, such as Helios and John Heathcoat, continued successfully to commission textile designs from artists for the wartime export drive, it was the lead taken by Zika and Lida Ascher which brought the concept of artist-designed textiles to full fruition. The Aschers arrived in Britain in 1939, following Germany's annexation of their home country, Czechoslovakia.

They brought with them an abundance of energy and enthusiasm and a sophisticated familiarity with, and understanding of, European Modernist art and culture. All of this necessarily stood them in good stead when setting up a small company in wartime London for the production of high quality textiles aimed at the couture end of the fashion market.

The London haute couture trade was then surprisingly thriving, largely the result of the cutting off of the Parisian couture houses from international markets by the German occupation of France in 1940. This eliminated any competition for the British industry in supplying the still prosperous markets of North and South America, where a successful export drive was not only a way of earning desperately needed dollars, but also a useful weapon of propaganda.

The leading British couturier, Edward Molyneux, evacuated his Paris-based couture house to London in 1940 where the government, seeking to exploit his international reputation, gave him official backing and financial aid to design both exclusive couture collections, for the export market, and economical ranges for the official wartime Utility Clothing Scheme. It was Molyneux who provided much needed patronage to the Aschers by buying most of Lida's first range of Modernist fashion textiles for his 1942 couture collection, a patronage he continued throughout the war.

In 1943 Zika Ascher commissioned his company's first textile designs by artists from the sculptor Henry Moore and the émigré Polish painter Feliks Topolski. Beyond limiting the size of a headscarf to a thirty-six inch square, he gave the artists involved carte blanche in their choice of subject matter. Although some of Ascher's artist-designed textiles had been available from 1944, they were not widely known until 1946, when the company showed part of the range at the first major British post-war exhibition of design, 'Britain Can Make It'. Organised by the newly formed Council of Industrial Design, the exhibition was held in London's Victoria and Albert Museum, then empty of most of its collections which had been evacuated for the duration of the war. Eventually Ascher's artists' range was extended to include not only headsquares and fashion fabrics, but also a series of silk screen-printed wall hangings designed by Henri Matisse and Henry Moore, which remain a high point in the twentieth century involvement of artists with textile design.

The project was undoubtedly an artistic triumph and a successful publicity coup, which served to kick-start the company into top gear at the end of the war. This success was further endorsed in the autumn of 1947, when the company exhibited a collection of thirty-seven headsquares by leading British and French artists at the Lefevre Gallery, London.[4] Clever marketing of the collection resulted in a great deal of publicity and media coverage, and the exhibition proved a winner. The Aschers further exploited this success by taking the exhibition to New York in October of the same year, following which it toured internationally, visiting venues in the Americas, Europe, Australia and South Africa.[5]

Zika and Lida Ascher were not the only ones then involved in the British textile industry who followed the pre-war examples of Allan Walton and Alastair Morton. The work of Hans and Elsbeth Juda was of particular significance for the successful post-war involvement of British artists with textile design. The Judas left Germany for Britain in 1933 after Hans had been obliged to stand up to Nazi Brownshirts in an incident in a Berlin cafe.[6] On arrival in Britain he was appointed editor of a Dutch owned magazine, *International Textiles*, of which he subsequently became proprietor at the end of the Second World War, and renamed *The Ambassador*. The importance of the Judas' role in the textile industry in the 1950s and 1960s was largely due to the influence of this highly regarded magazine for the export trade, although they also consistently primed and encouraged the general situation in the British industry throughout the difficulties and shortages of the 1940s.

A particularly close friend of the Judas was the painter Graham Sutherland, whose considerable involvement with textile design in the 1940s was very much inspired and encouraged by them. Throughout the war Sutherland served as an official war artist and was considered a leading light of the British neo-Romantic school of painting. Like Henry Moore, who followed a similar path at that time, Sutherland was not only involved with the design of textiles but also wallpapers[7] and illustrations for books and magazines. In 1946 nine of his textiles, designed for six companies, including Ascher, Helios and John Heathcoat, were exhibited at 'Britain Can Make It'[8] (Plate 3).

Another artist whose work was exhibited at 'Britain Can Make It' was the painter and critic Patrick Heron, who designed an outstanding textile, 'Aztec', for display at the exhibition by his father's company 'Cresta Silks'. The extraordinarily advanced design of 'Aztec', a printed spun rayon dress fabric, was prescient of the most accomplished pattern designs of the following decade[9] (Plate 4).

3 Opposite 'White Trellis', an artist's square designed by Graham Sutherland for Ascher Ltd, 1946. Screen-printed rayon. A version of this scarf and a companion design were exhibited by Ascher at 'Britain Can Make It', 1946, alongside Henry Moore's 'Standing Figures' and yardage by Gerald Wilde.

4 Anon, 'The First Exhibition of Artist Designed Squares', Lefevre Gallery, 1947.

5 Mendes and Hinchcliffe, *Ascher: Fabric, Art, Fashion*, V&A Publications, 1987.

6 Elsbeth Juda, interview with the authors, January 2002.

7 Exhibition catalogue, 'Historical & British Wallpapers', Suffolk Galleries, London, organised by the Central Institute of Art & Design, National Gallery, London 1945, pp. 43-44.

8 'Britain Can Make It', Catalogue of Exhibits, the Council of Industrial Design, Victoria & Albert Museum, HMSO, London 1946, pp. 25-31.

9 Ibid. p. 26, Group K, Dress Fabrics, no. 55.

In 1949 Sutherland received an important commission for textile designs from Horrockses Fashions, a subsidiary of the Lancashire based cotton manufacturer Horrockses, Crewdson & Company Ltd, for whom the Director of the Cotton Board's Manchester Centre, James Cleveland Belle, had been appointed design consultant. Cleveland Belle's position at the Cotton Board gave him a wide influence in the textile industry, allowing him to take a leading role in the selection of textiles and fashion for the 'Britain Can Make It' exhibition in 1946. This powerful status, combined with his many contacts and interests in the arts, enabled him to introduce to Horrockses a number of influential artists and fashion designers who would make a major contribution to the company's outstanding success in the later 1940s and 1950s. It was in this dual service to art and fashion that Cleveland Belle enlisted the formidable talents of the doyen of pre-war textiles in Britain, Alastair Morton, and, a little later, those of Sutherland.

Although, with the onset of war, most manufacturing activity at Morton's Edinburgh Weavers had ground to a halt, his poor physical health excluded him from active war service and he spent part of the war studying at the Ditchling studio of the leading British Modernist weaver, Ethel Mairet. In 1946 Edinburgh Weavers marked their post-war debut at 'Britain Can Make It' with a display of Morton's 'Unit Print' textiles. However his time was not completely taken up by Edinburgh Weavers, and he was also able to design for Horrockses Fashions: a situation which continued until 1954 when his growing workload for Edinburgh Weavers obliged him to give up any other commitments. The appointments of Morton and Sutherland, and that of Edward Molyneaux's cousin and former assistant, the fashion designer John Tullis, enabled Cleveland Belle to realise his idealistic ambitions for Horrockses Fashions in the 1950s.

4 Above 'Aztec', a dress textile designed by the painter Patrick Heron for Cresta Silks circa 1945, and printed for them by Thomas Wardle Ltd. Aztec was exhibited at the Victoria and Albert Museum's 'Britain Can Make It', 1946.

5 Opposite Dress yardage designed by Feliks Topolski for Ascher Ltd, circa 1945. For this textile, and others produced by Ascher, Topolski, an official war artist, used elements from his wartime sketchbooks. Zika Ascher's great skill was in being able to convey the vitality of Topolski's drawings to the resulting print

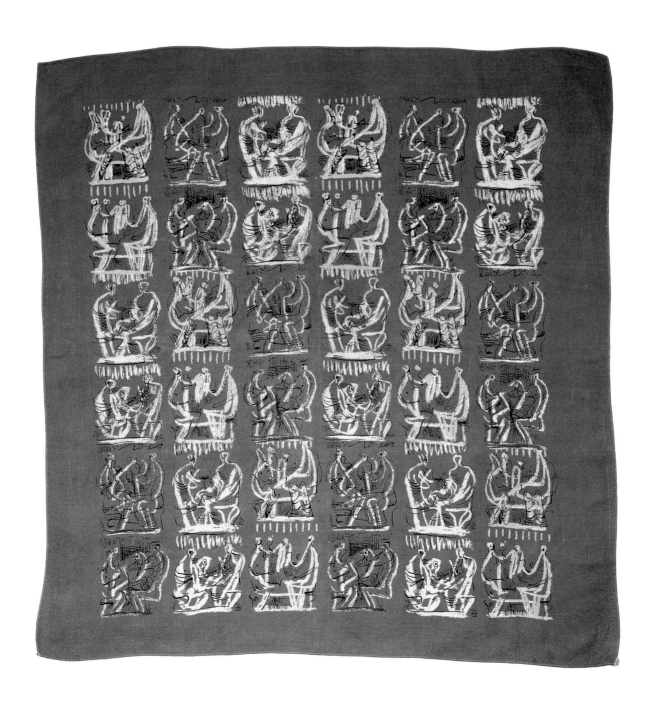

6 'Family Group', an artist's square designed by Henry Moore for Ascher, was exhibited both at 'Britain Can Make It', 1946, and the Lefevre Gallery, 1947, as well as being used for the cover of Grace Lovat Fraser's book, *Textiles by Britain*, 1948. The original sketches for the square date from circa 1944.

7 Henry Moore's artist's square, 'Bird', screen-printed onto silk, 1945. A trial colour proof for the intended limited edition of 375 produced in orange and grey. The origins of this design remain a mystery, as no related studies or drawings survive. It is thought that inspiration might have come from the book, *Indian Art of the United States*, which illustrates three versions of a bird with outstretched wings; Moore had a copy of this book in his library.

8 Right The artist's square 'Sans Bourne', by the French painter Francis Picabia, was printed onto a rayon crêpe and was one of 37 scarves to be exhibited at the Lefevre Gallery in 1947. Additional information to the exhibition catalogue suggested, 'Ascher Squares as wall decorations of great value ... the Aschers are opening up many new ways in which these works of art can be used.'

9 Opposite Christian Bérard, 'Les Elégantes' 1947, a dress fabric printed on both rayon crêpe and silk.

10 One of the three artists' squares that André Derain designed for Ascher that were exhibited at the Lefevre in 1947. This particular design, 'Écharpe No.3' was screen-printed onto silk twill.

11 'Visage', by Jean Cocteau,
for Ascher, screen-printed on
silk twill.

12 Jean Hugo's square
'Imprévisible Jeunesse',
screen-printed silk twill, 1947.
Ascher also exhibited Hugo's
square 'Fighting Centaurs' at
the Lefevre Gallery exhibition.

13 Alexander Calder, 'La Mer',
1947, for Ascher. Terence
Conran recalls helping to
print some of Ascher's artists
squares and Matisse's wall
hangings at Anton Eisler's
print studio whilst a student
at Central School in the 1940s.

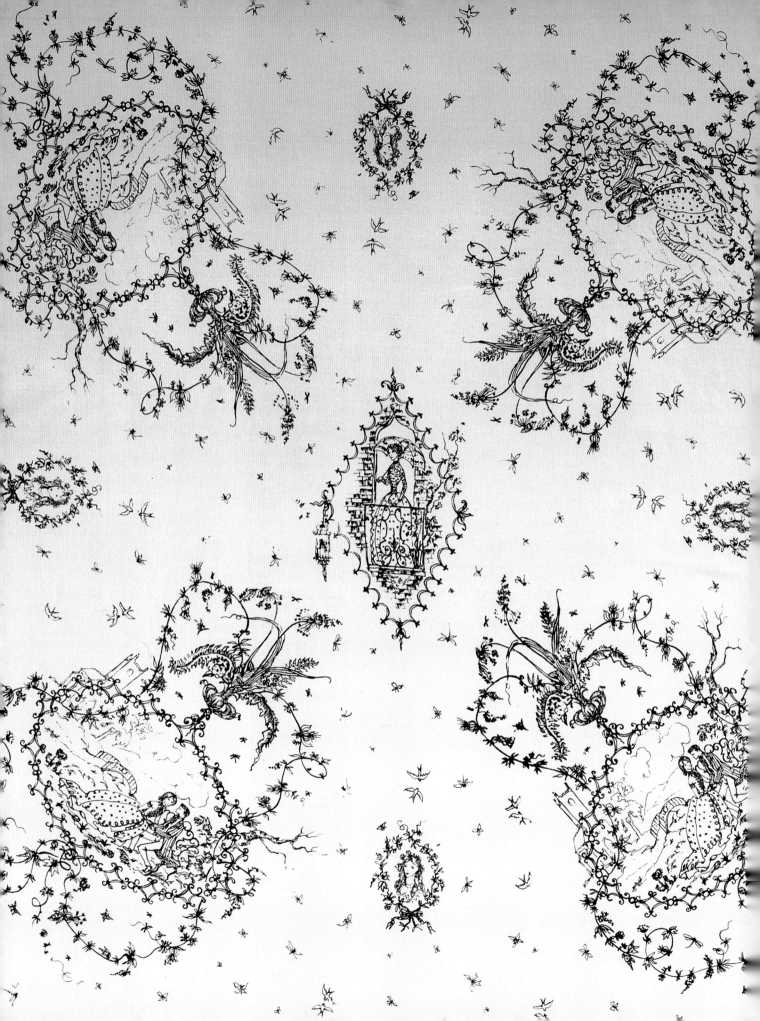

14 Opposite Fashion fabric by Phillippe Julian for Ascher, circa 1948.

15 Right 'Romantique', a "garden party" dress by Christian Dior, also using Julian's Ascher fabric, 1950. Photograph by Willy Maywald.

16 Opposite Henri Matisse's
first design for Ascher,
'Echarpe No. 1', was exhibited
at the Lefevre Gallery, 1947.
One of two coral-based
designs, it was intended to be
produced in a limited edition
of 275.

17 Next spread Fashion textile by Gerald Wilde for John
Heathcoat & Co., screen-printed silk, circa 1946. Wilde's
vibrant design was first shown at a Cotton Board exhibition
in 1944 and subsequently displayed by Heathcoat's at
'Britain Can Make It.'

18 'Moonlight', 1947,
Ben Nicholson's artist's
square printed by Ascher
on silk in an edition of 225.
Courtesy of H. Kirk Brown III
and Jill A. Wiltse.

19 'Landscape Sculpture',
Barbara Hepworth's artist's
square for Ascher, 1947,
was printed on a silk twill
and exhibited at the Lefevre
exhibition of the same year.
It was intended to be printed
in a limited edition of 175.

20 **Left** 'Gourmet' a screen-printed silk scarf designed by Patrick Heron for Cresta Silks, 1947. Cresta was run by Patrick's father Tom Heron, previously manager of Alec Walker's Cryséde Ltd. Patrick Heron designed many scarves and textiles for Cresta, his earliest, 'Melon', in 1934. Courtesy of H. Kirk Brown III and Jill A. Wiltse.

21 **Opposite** Printed cotton dress by Horrockses Fashions, made from a textile designed by Graham Sutherland, circa 1949, and featured in both *Tatler* and *The Queen*. Sutherland's work with textiles was extensive, from carpets in the 1940s through to scarf designs for Hardy Amies in the 1960s.

COHAMA MODERN

wonderful...workable

Made for modern furnishings--delightful
new abstractions in place of the
usual tropical flowers. Seven inspired
designs by talented Angelo Testa...plus th
plain colors you need for correlation.
Wonderful for drapes--and for upholster
too. Cohama has woven its usual fine
quality into them. And the price
is about one-third what you've had to
pay for fabrics of this character.
See them now in drapery departments.

*Cohama Upholstery and Drapery Fabr.
40 East 34th Street, New York...a divis
United Merchants and Manufacturers,*

America: Wesley Simpson Inc.: Salvador Dali and Marcel Vertes. Schiffer Prints: Salvador Dali. Angelo Testa & Company; Ben Rose Inc.; Laverne Originals

The 1940s was probably the most fruitful decade in America for the engagement of fine artists with the textile industry. The reasons for this were many, but reinforcing all of these was the enormous vitality, and enthusiasm, generated in the resurgence of American society and culture in the post-war era and the resultant openness to new ideas.

By the early 1940s interest in the fine arts in the United States had steadily grown far beyond that of the cultural elite usually interested in such things. This was, in part, a result of the multitudinous public art programmes organised in the previous decade by the Federal Art Project, the cultural branch of President Franklin D Roosevelt's New Deal programme, the Work Projects Administration, (WPA). While the cultural activities of the WPA contributed considerably, the work of many others, such as that of the artist and textile designer Ruth Reeves, also furthered this growing public interest in the arts. Of particular importance in this respect was the example of Associated American Artists, (AAA), a gallery founded in 1934 by an artists' agent, former journalist and PR man, Reeves Lewenthal.

During the Great Depression of the 1930s the activities of the Federal Art Project resulted in the production of thousands of artists' prints which were distributed free to institutions such as schools and colleges, a situation that gave the artists exposure but little or no financial return for their work. Lewenthal quickly realised that this situation, if effectively exploited and organised with the cooperation of the artists concerned, would allow AAA to offer original signed artists' etchings and lithographs, at extremely affordable prices, to a potentially vast and largely untapped middle-class market.

By late 1934 Lewenthal had contracted with fifty department stores across the country to carry AAA's range of artists' prints, which he simultaneously marketed directly to the public by mail order through magazines such as *Time* and *Reader's Digest*. The artists under contract to Lewenthal received $200 for each edition, and AAA become an agent of economic salvation, whilst simultaneously creating a uniquely American version of 'art for the people' through a synthesis of art, business and consumerism.

In 1941 the country entered the Second World War and reassurance of the survival and continuity of traditional American ways of life and values became as essential for the nation's

22 Magazine advertisement for Cohama Upholstery & Drapery Fabrics, February 1947, illustrating three fabrics by Angelo Testa, including a version of his 'Little Man' textile, initially created for a class assignment at the Institute of Design in Chicago in 1942.

Contemporary American Artists Prints
Great Art transposed on *pure silks.*

Styled by *Philip A. Vogelman*

Sophie Original in
Jardin aux Lilas print

ONONDAGA SILK COMPANY

The Artists
JULIEN BINFORD
DORIS ROSENTHAL
WALDO PEIRCE
DONG KINGMAN
WILLIAM PALMER
GLADYS ROCKMORE DAVIS

23 Advertisement for Onondaga Silk Company's 'Contemporary American Artists Prints', 1947.

[10] Erika Doss, 'Catering to Consumerism: Associated American Artists and the marketing of Modern Art 1934-1958,' *Winterthur Portfolio*, vol. 26, no. 2/3, autumn/summer 1991.

[11] Walter Abell, 'Industry and Painting', *Magazine of Art*, March 1946.

[12] Dilys Blum, 'Post-War American Textiles' in *Surreal Things, Surrealism and Design*, ed. Ghislaine Wood, V&A Publications, London 2007, p. 240.

[13] René Simon Lévy, 'The Fabrics of Raoul Dufy', essay first published in exhibition catalogue *Raoul Dufy*, ed. Bryan Robertson and Sarah Wilson, Arts Council of Great Britain, Hayward Gallery, London, 9 November 1983-5 February 1986, p.106.

[14] Nikolaus Pevsner, 'Can Painters Design Textiles?' *Art In Industry*, vol.1, no.1, Calcutta, December 1946, pp.11-17.

morale as romance and glamour. Since the late 1930s fine art had been increasingly used as a marketing tool by industrial and corporate America and, with the advent of war, was also co-opted by the Federal Government as a powerful propaganda weapon. Plugging into this patriotic zeitgeist many advertising and PR agencies chose the work of representational and regional artists with a wide populist appeal for their clients' campaigns and corporate identities. These artists created positive images of an idealized, strong and capable America, which not only accorded well with the needs of big business but also with those of the government, which successfully appropriated the regionalist/representational style for wartime propaganda posters.

This marriage of art with commerce and propaganda financially underwrote the activities of many mainstream art galleries in the 1940s. These galleries promoted the careers of their artists by encouraging the formation of corporate art collections, for publicity purposes, and the commissioning of new work for use in advertising campaigns, such as that commissioned from Georgia O'Keeffe by Dole Pineapple to 'create pictorial links between pineapple juice and tropical romance'.[10] The impact of this widespread commercialisation of art led the art critic Walter Abell to write, in 1946:

"Today industry appears to have established itself as the largest single source of support for the contemporary American painter."[11]

The earlier cultural activities of the Federal Art Project and the commercialisation of art by galleries such as Associated American Artists, in tandem with big business and department stores, helped create a receptive climate amongst the public in the early post-war years for art in a wide variety of guises. This fast growing interest was further reinforced through exhibitions held by institutions such as New York's Metropolitan Museum of Art and the Museum of Modern Art.

"By mid-1949 the United States was flooded with exhibitions exploring the influence of modern art on contemporary living, including the influential Museum of Modern Art's twentieth anniversary exhibition, 'Modern Art in Your Life', which displayed more than a hundred examples of architecture, industrial design, advertising and window displays derived from twentieth century art forms."[12]

Increasingly, owning modern art, in whatever form, became seen as a social asset.

Since the work of the Fauvist painter Raoul Dufy for the French textile manufacturer Bianchini-Férier in the early twentieth century, the involvement of avant-garde European artists with textile design had long been an accepted

part of their oeuvre. In comparison, in America, other than Ruth Reeves, there had been few similar examples. One exception was the ill-fated collaboration between the New York based Onondaga Silk Company and Dufy in the early 1930s.[13]

In 1946 Onondaga became involved once more with an artists' textile project 'Contemporary American Artists Prints': the brain child of Alan Gruskin, director of the Midtown Gallery, New York. Like Associated American Artists, Gruskin's Midtown Gallery was one of a number of American art galleries which advocated the commercial use of fine art by corporate business. The work of the six painters selected by Gruskin for the Midtown/Onondaga textile project was solidly mainstream and representational – described at the time as 'American scene' styles of painting. In 1946 Nikolaus Pevsner wrote that since art had moved away from narrow representational concerns there was a greater chance of success for the involvement of artists in textile design.[14] However, in this instance, it was the representational style that dominated. On completion the range was given the full razzamatazz of a Gruskin promotion with a travelling exhibition, which included examples of the textiles used for dresses by New York designers, and the entire project documented on film. This commercial promotion and exploitation of art by galleries like AAA and Midtown, in collaboration with 'big business', was something very much of its time.

In Britain the equally ambitious Lida and Zika Ascher were also vigorously promoting their company's range of fashion textiles designed by internationally renowned artists; their exhibition of artist-designed headsquares arriving in New York in 1947. The venture was, however, unlike that of the Midtown/Onondaga collaboration, entirely their own and the modernity of the designs made no concessions to popular prejudice. Zika Ascher personally commissioned the artists involved and the resulting textiles were produced in the Ascher workshops, often in collaboration with the artist concerned. This had long been the practice in Europe, where textile manufacturers usually initiated such projects and directly commissioned designs from artists.

During the 1940s some American companies also began to deal directly with artists; probably the first was the New York-based textile converter, Wesley Simpson Custom Fabrics Inc., founded at the height of the depression around 1933. From the end of the war the company embarked on an extensive promotional campaign. This was a two-pronged strategy, carried out through both newspaper advertisements, which linked the sale of Wesley Simpson Fabrics with the home dressmaking market and a particular department store in a given city, and by advertisements carefully placed in prestigious magazines such as *Vogue* and *Harper's Bazaar*, which associated Simpson fabrics with the better American designers and dress houses. By March 1947 Simpson had a customer list of some 350 retail stores throughout the country.[15] It was probably as part of this campaign that Simpson directly commissioned designs for fashion yardage and scarves from a number of avant-garde artists, the most eminent of whom were Salvador Dali and Marcel Vertes.

Although Hungarian by birth, Vertes had worked mainly in France as a painter, muralist and internationally celebrated illustrator. His first work for Wesley Simpson appeared in 1942 in the 6th October issue of *Women's Wear Daily*, in an article announcing Simpson's launch of his Vertes designed textiles. Shortly after, an advertisement for four Vertes scarves appeared in the November 1942 issue of *Harper's Bazaar*. Probably the first, and certainly the most prolific of the artists commissioned by Simpson, Vertes produced over sixty textile designs and six scarves for the company between 1942 and 1948.[16]

In 1946 Simpson commissioned Dali to design at least six textiles and some nine scarves, under the Surrealist banner, for the 'Wesley Simpson's Artist Series'. First advertised in early 1947, Dali's surreal designs reflect those of his dream sequence for Alfred Hitchcock's 1945 film *Spellbound*, which the American public would have been familiar with. Hollywood became further involved when costume and fashion designer to the stars, Adrian, used Dali fabrics for two stunning evening dresses, one of which was the extraordinary 'Desert Rocks'; the dresses appeared in *Vogue*, April, 1947, in advertisements that credit Wesley Simpson Custom Fabrics, Inc. The design for one of his scarves, 'Number Please?' was a further Hollywood connection: it was taken from a sequence for Dali's unfinished animation, *Destino*, for Walt Disney, 1946. The textiles and Dali's original designs for them were also exhibited the same year in New York at the Cooper Union Museum for the Arts of Decoration, now the Cooper Hewitt National Design Museum.

Vertes took part in a further textile project in the later 1940s, the conception of an artist's agent and freelance art consultant, Stephan Lion, who represented some nine

24 Detail of 'Flower Ballet' a textile designed by Salvador Dali, circa 1947, printed by Wesley Simpson on their 'Pebble Crêpe' rayon, giving this design a further surreal aspect.

[15] Lynn Felsher, 'Wesley Simpson: Designer, Converter and Entrepreneur,' a paper given at the Textile Society of America Symposium, 2002.

[16] Ibid.

25 **Below** A printed wall
hanging depicting the design
and manufacturing process
for a block print, by Folly
Cove Designers, 1940s.

26 **Opposite** 'Gossips',
a furnishing textile designed
by Virginia Lee Burton
(Demitrios) and printed by
the Folly Cove Designers,
1940s.

[17] Anon, editorial in *American
Fabrics*, no. 9, 1949, Doric
Publishing Co. Inc., New York.

leading artists, as well as the Knoedler Gallery
and their stable of painters. Other artists who
took part in Lion's project were Cecil Beaton,
Eugene Berman, Jean Pages, and Jean De Botton,
although he had to overcome much scepticism
and resistance before he was able to convince
them to work with him to create original
textile designs.

"The difference between Lion's approach and existing technics lay in the fact that Lion
worked with his group of artists to create new and especially designed ideas, rather than
reproduce literally from paintings which had been conceived as paintings to be hung."[17]

The project resulted in a successful range
of high quality furnishing and dress fabrics
produced by Stoffel, and promoted as 'The Artist
Paints in Print'.

Lion's was one of a number of small-scale
projects that emerged in the
burgeoning market for artist-designed
textiles in the late 1940s. Another was
'Contempora', an artists' cooperative,
which, between 1947 and 1949,
produced ranges of scarves and ties
under the guidance of the British
master print maker Stanley William
Hayter. Amongst the artists whose
work he oversaw in his New York
Studio, Atelier 17, was the painter
and textile designer Ruth Reeves.

A project much in sympathy
with Reeves's design philosophy was
The Folly Cove Designers, a collective
of designer-craftspeople set up in 1939
by the artist and illustrator Virginia
Lee Burton, in Gloucester,
Massachusetts. Burton was one of the
most significant American children's
book illustrators of the twentieth
century and it was a natural
development of her work with block
printed illustration that led her to
textile printing and design. As a textile
designer and printer she worked
under the name of Virginia Demetrios,
and, for the group of local people who
comprised The Folly Cove Designers,
she proved a dynamic and gifted
teacher, developing an extremely
effective, comprehensive, but simple,
system of teaching for those without
any art training.

The collective produced
sophisticated and detailed textiles and
quickly achieved a remarkable degree
of commercial success. By the fall of
1941 their work was being sold in
New York by America House, and
subsequently in stores throughout the

27 a, b and c Three from the
group of four screen-printed
rayon headsquares designed
by Marcel Vertes
for Wesley Simpson Custom
Fabrics Inc., circa 1944.

28 Next page left 'Picadilly' (*sic*), printed cotton designed
by Angelo Testa for Cohama, late 1940s.

29 Next page right Hand screen-printed furnishing
textile, designed and printed by Angelo Testa circa 1947.
This perfect example of Testa's early 'line in action' style
illustrates the thinking behind his spatial concepts. In an
interview in *Art & Architecture*, 1946, he explained that
'by the use of thick and thin lines, combinations of solid
and outline forms, a freer articulation of positive and
negative space is brought into play.'

United States of America. In 1945 The Folly Cove Designers received the accolade of having six of their designs bought for silkscreen production by Schumacher, the doyen of American textile manufacturers. In November of that year a feature on the cooperative's work appeared in *Life* magazine announcing the forthcoming sale of their textiles for Schumacher 'in at least 14 leading department stores throughout the country'.[18] The collective continued to prosper until 1969, when, following Virginia Lee Burton's death the previous year, the members decided to wind the venture up.

In the second half of the 1940s in Chicago, two important and long-lived studios and workshops for textile design and production were set up by the painters Angelo Testa and Ben Rose, both graduates of the city's celebrated art educational establishments.

Originally a painter and sculptor, Testa had studied at Chicago's Institute of Design, founded by the former Bauhaus Master, László Moholy-Nagy. He was to become one of the most successful American textile designers of the twentieth century. Although his best-known work, more influenced by Modernist design theory than painterly and expressive values, was especially favoured by the elite of the American Modernist establishment, such as Knoll Associates, Herman Miller, Jens Risom and the Museum of Modern Art, this had not always been the case. His early designs, many made while still a student in the 1940s, often display a wit and expressionist energy which is far less apparent in his later more reductive, architecturally-influenced work. From the start Testa successfully combined the creation of unique hand screen-printed wall hangings with his core operation: the production of furnishing fabrics for the mass market. He also designed carpets, wallpapers and plastic laminates, as well as textiles for some of the most prestigious American manufacturers, including F Schumacher & Company and Greef Fabrics. Possibly the first to produce a range of his designs, in 1947, including his celebrated 1942 design 'Little Man', was Cohama (Cohn-Hall-Marx), a division of United Merchants and Manufacturers Inc.

In 1946 Testa's principal competitor, the painter Ben Rose, also set up a studio and manufactory for the design and production of textiles. Between 1939 and 1941 Rose studied painting and illustration at the School of Fine Art of the Art Institute of Chicago, until his studies were interrupted by the Second World War and he was drafted into the United States Navy. At the end of the war he planned to resume his

studies at the Art Institute but found all places filled, and it was while waiting for a vacancy to occur that he unexpectedly found himself commissioned to produce 3000 yards of textile. The commission came from an architect friend who had received a set of place mats designed and screen-printed by Rose as Christmas gifts in 1945. He needed a large quantity of modern curtain material for a building he was designing and decided the mats' abstract designs were ideal for the purpose. The resulting commission was a godsend to Rose and his wife and, before it was even completed, they had received a second commission from another architect, and orders began to come in thick and fast.

Rose's business flourished, and for nearly fifty years he was pre-eminent amongst progressive American textile manufacturers, with showrooms in New York and Chicago and his work was promoted by other distinguished textile companies such as L Anton Maix. His remarkable success was recognised in his first season as a manufacturer, in 1946, when he was given a prestigious award for textile design by the influential American Institute of Decorators. In 1952 he received a further three awards for textiles and wallpapers from the Institute, one of which was for 'Foliation', the inspiration for many similar designs, such as 'Fall', also from 1952, by the British designer Lucienne Day. Rose's particular achievement was to evolve successfully a Modern design idiom which, while retaining painterly and expressive values, chimed easily with the aesthetics of Modernist interiors.

A more extreme example of the involvement of artists with design was that of the New York-based painters Estelle and Erwine Laverne, who, throughout their working lives, were uncompromising in their commitment to the merger of the fine and applied arts in the production of wallpapers, textiles and furniture. They had first met at the Art Students League in 1934, and although they worked together from that time, it was not until 1942 that they founded Laverne Originals as a commercial vehicle for their ideas concerning the integration of fine art with design.

30 Opposite 'Harvest Time', designed by the painter, print maker and illustrator Rockwell Kent for 'The Happily Married' collection of furnishing textiles, produced by Bloomcraft Inc, 1950.

31 Above 'Foliation' a furnishing textile designed and hand-printed by Ben Rose, 1951. Widely illustrated in contemporary international design journals, such as the *Studio Yearbook of Decorative Art*, 'Foliation' had a huge influence on contemporary textile design in Britain, particularly designers such as Lucienne Day and Terence Conran.

18 Folly Cove Designers, Yankee Prints Get National Recognition,' in *Life* magazine, 26 November 1945, pp. 80-82.

Their prestigious showroom in New York, which left no doubt as to their purpose, had none of the obvious markers that denote a retail establishment; it was more 'a dazzling statement of their specific mission ... a whisper of a showroom.'[19]

"... you might conceivably enter the room at the left, make a cursory search for showroom signposts, and finding only a dangling sculpture and a bench or two, conclude you are in a museum. It seems too fragile, too pure, to support any mundane transactions like selling items to decorators. Actually, the museum-like quality is a direct expression of what the Lavernes are selling: not just designs (although everything is Original, and for sale) but a concrete effort to relate fine and applied arts, business be darned."[20]

The 'dangling sculpture' was in fact a mobile by the sculptor Alexander Calder, who had from early on designed coordinated wallpapers and textiles for the Laverne's 'Contempora' range, such as the wryly-named 'Splotchy' of 1949. Calder was one of a group of artists, architects, illustrators and designers who designed for Laverne Originals some of the most influential American textiles and furniture of the post-war era. Included amongst these were the architects William Katavolos and Oscar Niemeyer; industrial designers Ross Littell and Douglas Kelley, and graphic designers Ray Komai and Alvin Lustig. One of the best known of Estelle Laverne's textile designs, the clever and amusing 'Fun to Run', 1948, was also for the 'Contempora' range (Plate 33).

Another company that commissioned an assortment of Modernist architects and industrial designers to create a Modern textile range was Schiffer Prints. Perhaps incongruously included in the project was Salvador Dali, who, unlike the others, had a long and distinguished history of collaborating on textile projects, such as that with the fashion designer Elsa Schiaparelli in Paris in the 1930s, and later with Wesley Simpson.

Dali's five Surrealist prints for Schiffer stand in marked contrast to the strict Modernist aesthetic of the company's first 'Stimulus Collection', launched in 1949. Three of Dali's designs were included in the range: 'Beste Elenique', a classically inspired subject of horses and naked riders; 'Afternoon Stones', essentially a rehash of his successful 'Desert Rocks' and the third, a semi abstract design of musical instruments, 'Sonata d'Été'. Later that year Schiffer issued a second collection incorporating Dali's final two prints for them, 'Leaf Hands' and the remarkable 'Spring Rain', in which the vertebrae of a skeletal spine intermingle with abstracted raindrops and young green leaves. Dali's subversion of everyday reality through Surrealist design continued throughout the

1940s and 1950s, extending even to the design of ties, one of which, with the title, 'Endless Where?' bore the iconic image of melting clocks from his painting of 1931, *The Persistence of Memory*.

The multitude of artists' textile projects in Britain and America in the 1940s are exceptional for their diversity, richness and inventiveness, and equally the enthusiastic reception of the work by the public. Many painters and sculptors had laid the groundwork for a remarkable flowering of artist-designed textiles in the following decades by some of the greatest artists of the twentieth century.

32 Right 'Condiment', a printed fabric designed by Ben Rose for Ben Rose Textiles, circa 1950, exclusively for the International Harvester Company.

33 Opposite The husband and wife team of Estelle and Erwine Laverne, both painters, formed Laverne Originals in 1942. This furnishing textile, 'Fun to Run', was designed by Estelle for the company's 'Contempora' range in 1947.

[19] Anon, Interiors, March 1952, Whitney Publications, New York.

[20] Ibid.

34 'Number, Please?' a silk
scarf designed by Dali for
Wesley Simpson circa 1947.
The design is derived from a
sequence in Dali's animation
for Disney of 1946, *Destino*.

35 'Ballerina', a screen-printed silk scarf designed by Salvador Dali for Wesley Simpson circa 1947.

36 Screen-printed silk scarf designed by Salvador Dali for Wesley Simpson circa 1947. Dali created at least nine scarf designs and five textile designs for the company in the 1940s.

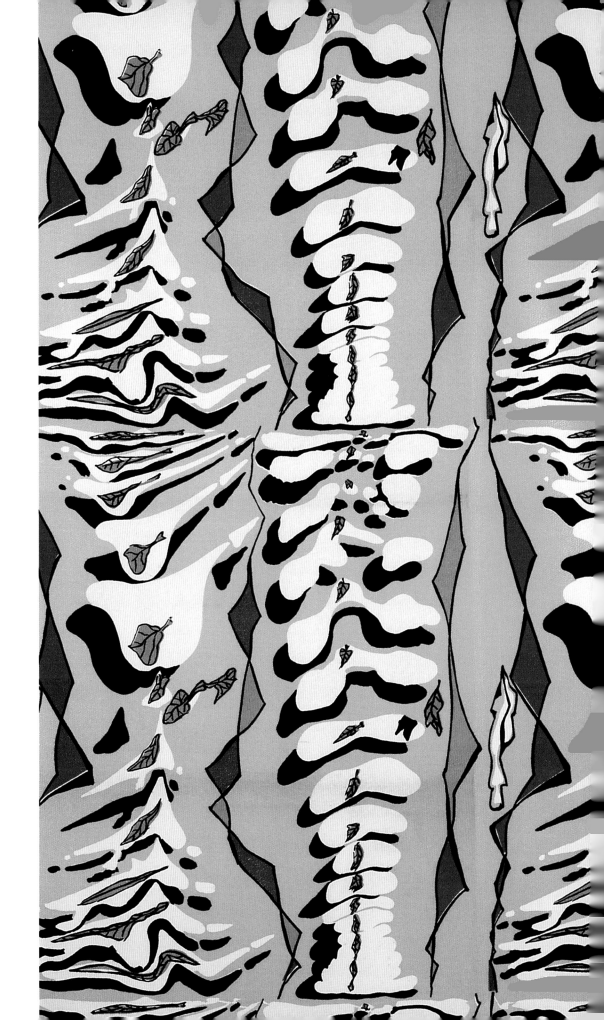

37 'Spring Rain' a furnishing textile from Schiffer Prints' second 'Stimulus' collection, 1949. Dali's surrealist designs of the 1940s had a wide influence on textile design in the USA for the next ten years.

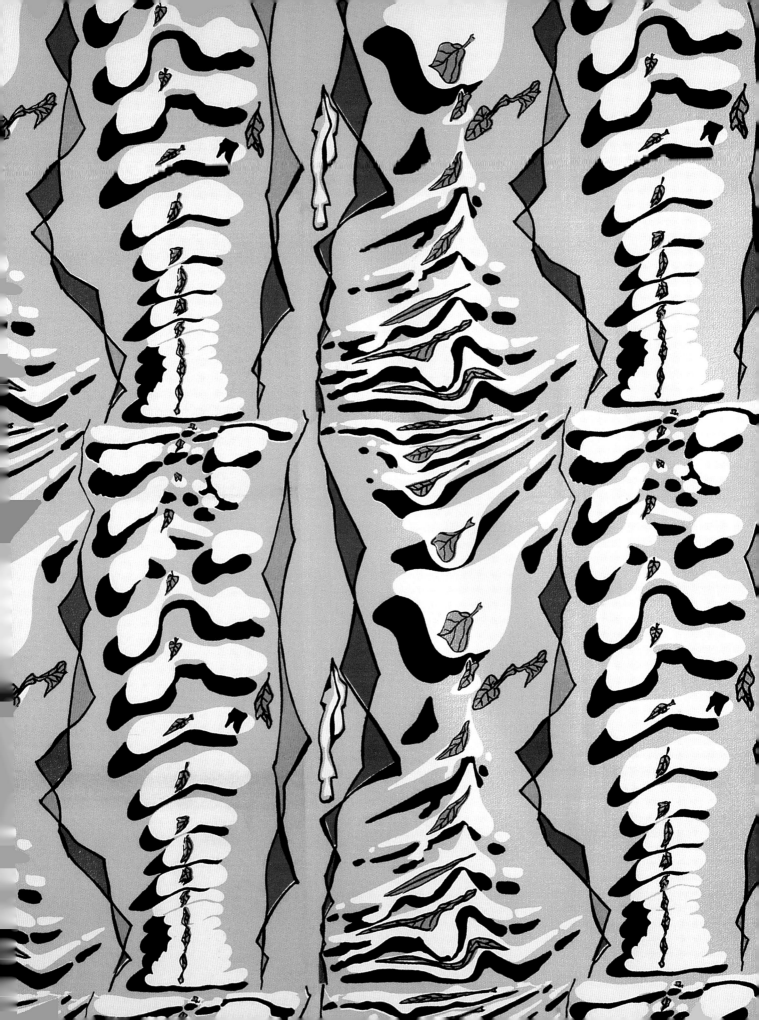

38 and 39 'Splotchy' designed
by Alexander Calder for
Laverne Originals, 1949.
Calder's designs for Laverne
Originals were produced both
as wallpapers and textiles.
They were marketed under
the 'Contempora' range
which also included the
work of graphic designer
Alvin Lustig and architect
Oscar Niemeyer.

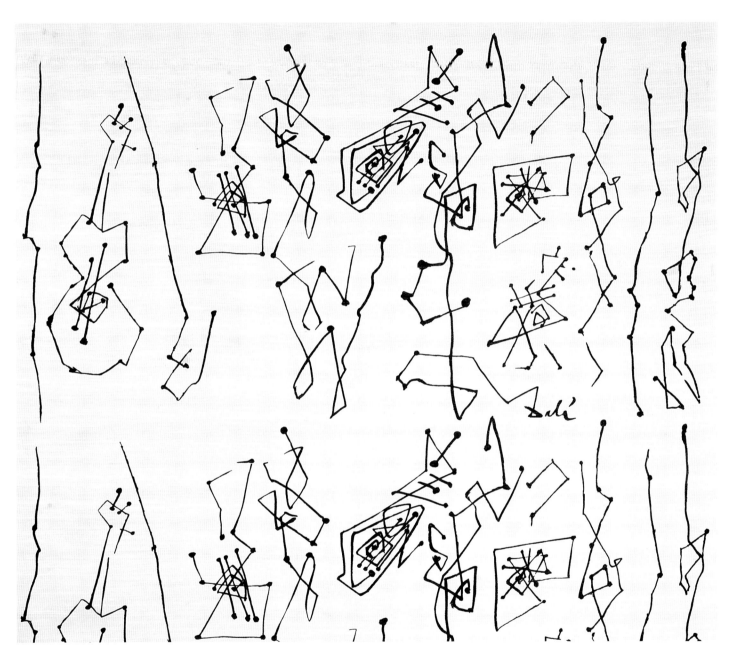

40 Opposite 'Endless - Where?'
a printed rayon tie designed
by Salvador Dali, late 1940s.
Dali created numerous tie
designs throughout the 1940s
for a number of companies.

41 Above 'Sonata d'Été'
a screen-printed sheer
furnishing fabric designed
by Salvador Dali for Schiffer
Prints' first 'Stimulus'
collection, 1949.

The 1950s witnessed the apogee of artist-designed textiles in America and Britain, with manufacturers in both countries persuading some of the most internationally eminent artists to take part in projects that elevated textile design to the status of high art.

Britain: 'Painting into Textiles', the Institute of Contemporary Arts (ICA), 1953; David Whitehead Ltd; Hammer Prints; Porthia Prints; Edinburgh Weavers; Louis Le Brocquy for John McGuire of Dublin, and the Iberian project for The Ambassador

In 1950 Picasso provided a magnificent curtain-raiser for the decade with the gift to his friend Roland Penrose, director of the ICA, of a design for a limited edition of a hundred silk headsquares to raise funds for the newly formed Institute. The 'Bulls and Sunflowers' design (Plate 3), originally drawn by Picasso in the ICA's visitors' book in 1950, was also used for a further limited edition of a hundred prints on paper, and the cover of the catalogue of the Institute's exhibition of Picasso's drawings, held to celebrate his seventieth birthday in 1951.

The country's major cultural event of the decade, the 'Festival of Britain', was also held in 1951. Yet, apart from the textiles designed by the painter Roger Nicholson for Heal & Son Ltd. and David Whitehead Ltd. and a fifty-foot long batik wall hanging by Michael O'Connell, few others by artists were in evidence in the Festival's displays. Textile design in Britain in the early 1950s was largely the province of professional designers, whose work was heavily influenced by the pseudoscientific imagery associated with the 'Festival of Britain' and by the work of painters and sculptors such as Joan Miró, Paul Klee and Jean Arp. By 1953 commercial exploitation had begun to debase the numerous popular designs derived from these sources and modern textile design was in danger of becoming trapped in an aesthetic cul-de-sac.

It was in response to this situation that Hans and Elsbeth Juda conceived the exhibition 'Painting into Textiles', a remarkably fruitful cooperation between the ICA and *The Ambassador* in 1953. Hans considered textile design an art form, a proposition he assiduously promoted throughout his thirty or so years tenure of the magazine which, following the end of the war, became the leading international export publication promoting not only the British textile industry but also British industries and culture. The Judas went out of their way to encourage young talent across the arts from painting and sculpture to ballet and opera. They commissioned designs and paintings from avant-garde artists, many of which were used for the magazine's cover, or lent to

1 **Opposite left** Catalogue cover for 'Painting into Textiles' exhibition at the Institute of Contemporary Arts, 1953. The design, 'Zig Zag', by Henry Moore, was also used as the cover of *The Ambassador*, issue no. 11 1953, which incorporated the exhibition catalogue. It was produced by David Whitehead Ltd as a textile in 1954.

2 **Opposite right** Roger Nicholson's screen-printed linen, 'Matura', for Heal & Son Ltd, was launched at the company's display at the Festival of Britain, 1951, and illustrated in the *Studio Yearbook of Decorative Art*, 1952-53', p. 78.

3 **Left** Headsquare with a design of bulls, suns and foliage by Pablo Picasso for the Institute of Contemporary Arts, 1950. An edition of a hundred, intended to raise funds for the Institute, was hand screen printed onto silk by Ascher Ltd.

manufacturers as sources for ideas and inspiration, accumulating an impressive art collection as a consequence. As enthusiastic supporters and patrons, and generous hosts, they numbered many artists among their close friends, including Joe Tilson, Henry Moore, John Piper, Louis Le Brocquy, Graham Sutherland and William Scott. Through the success of the magazine they were able to not only support artists directly but also to encourage other influential patrons, industrialists and enthusiasts of the arts.

Hans Juda felt it essential that artists involved in 'Painting into Textiles' showed original works of art rather than finished textile designs which manufacturers could then use as inspirations for designs or interpret directly as textiles. However the work of a number of established textile designers such as Jacqueline Groag, Marian Mahler and the young Pat Albeck, was included alongside that of artists like Graham Sutherland, who had been designing textiles since the mid-forties. The exhibition proved a great success with both manufacturers and the public, and brought about a wider appreciation of textile design as an appropriate medium for artistic expression.

Among those who used works from the exhibition to inspire textile design that added considerably to the prestige of the British industry, was David Whitehead Ltd. The large number of works purchased by this go-ahead company included paintings and drawings by William Scott, Henry Moore and, although not shown at the exhibition, a collage by Eduardo Paolozzi.[1] Their most successful collaboration with an artist was the translation of a group of works by John Piper, of which 'Foliate Head' might be considered the most significant (Plate 14); Piper continued to design for Whitehead until the company's closure in 1970.

James Cleveland Belle, another friend of the Judas, also used a number of art works from 'Painting into Textiles' for Horrockses Fashions. Perhaps the most outstanding was a mixed media design by Paolozzi that was directly translated as a fashion textile and used by John Tullis for a cocktail dress included in the Horrockses' collection from which the young Queen Elizabeth II selected items for her coronation tour of the Commonwealth.[2] Cleveland Belle's partner, Sir David Webster, was then General Administrator of the Royal Opera House, Covent Garden, and through this connection Horrockses Fashions gained much publicity when their dresses were worn by celebrities of the day, such as the prima ballerina Dame Margot Fonteyn and the Queen's sister,

4 'Triangles and Lines', a textile designed by Henry Moore and produced by David Whitehead Ltd, 1954. The artwork was exhibited at 'Painting into Textiles', 1953.

[1] This textile is the only one known by Paolozzi for David Whitehead Ltd but is not related to the two known pictures by the artist exhibited at 'Paintings into Textiles'. Although previously dated to 1952, a serial number attached to a sample swatch in the collection of the Whitworth Art Gallery, Manchester, places it in a sequence for 1954-55.

[2] *The Ambassador*, no. 12, 1953, p. 111.

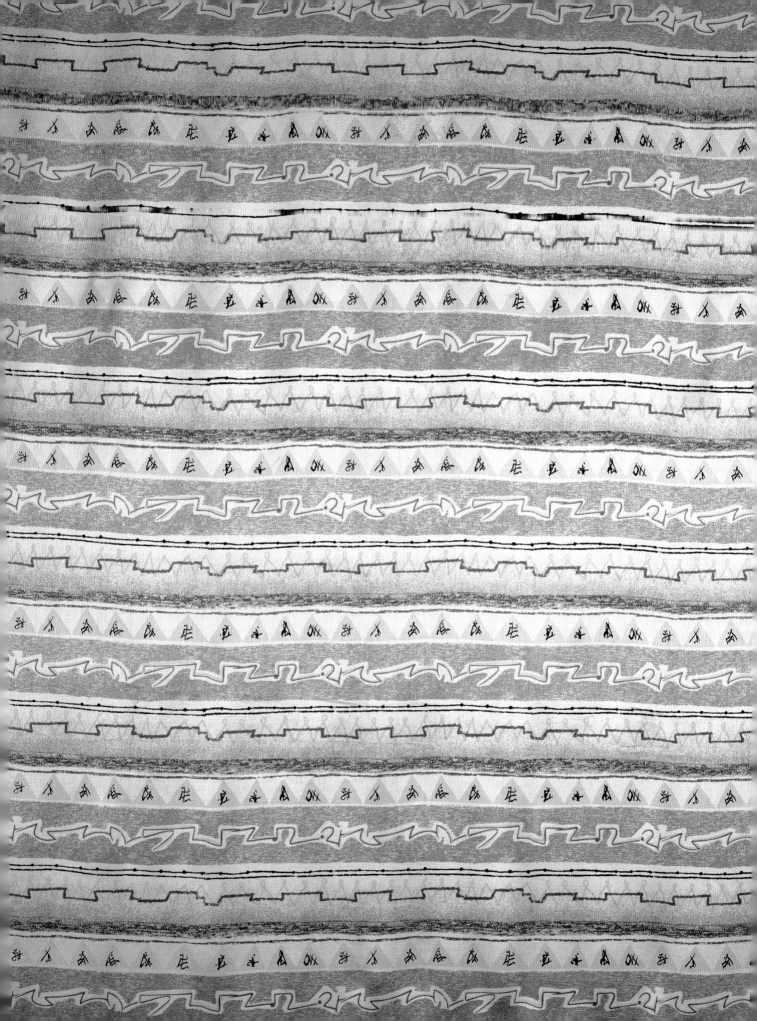

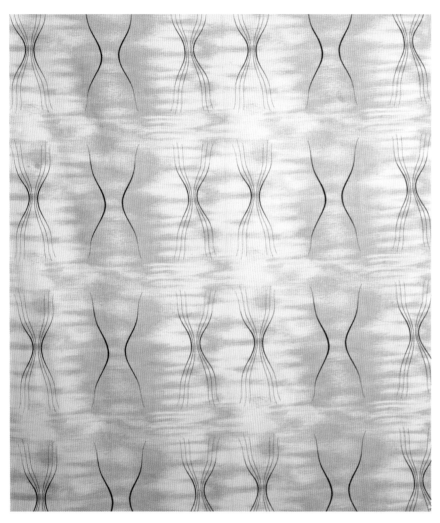

5 Above 'Elegance' designed by Paule Vézelay for Heals, circa 1955.

6 Opposite Furnishing textile designed by Robert Stewart for Liberty & Co. circa 1954. This design, like others by Stewart, was marketed under the 'Young Liberty' label alongside designs by the painter Martin Bradley and the designer Lucienne Day.

[3] Elsbeth Juda, interview with authors, September 2002.

[4] *The Ambassador*, no. 2, 1956, p. 87.

[5] 'Wassail', by Ben Nicholson, hand screen-printed cotton satin. *The Ambassador*, no. 3, 1956, p. 101.

Princess Margaret.[3] Other notable successes were two paintings by William Gear, translated by Horrockses Crewdson & Co. Ltd into dramatic furnishing statements, and William Turnbull's large scale drawing of a kinetic figure, used full length as a border print for skirts by the Berne Silk Manufacturing Co. Ltd.[4]

The lead given by 'Painting into Textiles' inspired many other manufacturers to commission work directly from artists, amongst whom were Heal & Son Ltd, who engaged the painter Paule Vézelay, and Liberty of London, who used the work of Martin Bradley and the Scottish painter and designer Robert Stewart.

One of the most significant spin-offs from the exhibition was the recommencing of the 'majestic' series of artist textiles by Edinburgh Weavers, under Alastair Morton's visionary direction. Morton used a painting by Gear to create 'Tropic' and quickly followed up with commissions to other artists, including Geoffrey Clarke, Kenneth Rowntree, Keith Vaughan and, once more, Ben Nicholson.[5] This powerful sequence of textiles was continued by Edinburgh Weavers throughout the 1950s.

In 1954 Eduardo Paolozzi and the avant-garde photographer Nigel Henderson set up Hammer Prints Ltd, which was to become an influential workshop for applied art. The same year Henderson and his wife Judith, an anthropologist and sociologist, moved to Thorpe-le-Soken in Essex, where they were joined by Paolozzi and his wife Freda, a textile designer. Their idea was to form an artists' cooperative that would encompass all aspects of interior design, from murals to furniture, textiles and ceramics. Until then, Paolozzi had lectured for a number of years on textile design at London's Central School of Arts and Crafts, and was particularly interested in the potential of silk screen printing. He and Henderson created patterns and designs for Hammer Prints from an eclectic assortment of photographic material and images derived from popular culture and ethnographic and scientific sources, which they mixed with an incongruous melange of found objects and ephemera. The resulting patterns were then silk-screened indiscriminately onto textiles, wallpapers, tiles and ceramics, creating some of the most radical and influential designs of the period in Britain.

'Barkcloth' is a quintessential Hammer Print interpretation of tribal textiles (Plate 11). Its name is derived from that of the cloth made in many tribal societies from the fibrous inner bark of trees, with its random pattern, as in a cargo cult, incorporating magically endowed objects from remote technologically advanced

societies, such as spectacles, bicycles, clocks, torches and cog wheels, randomly jumbled with insects and fossils, letters from the western alphabet and numerals, interspersed with faux tribal patterns. In many ways these richly layered, but incoherent, visual references, are analogous with the interest in western consumerist society of the intellectuals of the Independent Group – of which Paolozzi and Henderson were significant members – where consumers were often interpreted as passive recipients of a continual stream of sophisticated, but ill-understood, scientifically derived goods; an endless barrage of banal, disparate and increasingly meaningless, media driven images.

Judith and Nigel Henderson's early life at the centre of the Bloomsbury circle and her academic studies of anthropology and sociology had a profound influence on the way of life at Thorpe-le-Soken. Judith was the daughter of the psychoanalyst Adrian Stephen, brother of Vanessa Bell and Virginia Woolf. Similarly it was, through his very bohemian mother Wyn, that Henderson first came to know many of Bloomsbury's leading members, and from his youth was 'saturated in Bloomsbury history.'[6] Despite the sharpness of its cutting edge modernity, Hammer Prints' agenda was essentially that of Roger Fry's for the Omega Workshops. From the declared anonymity of the designs, to the amused snobbery and dilettantism of the Hendersons, and the general sense of recrimination between the partners on its demise in 1961, the venture was tinged with shades of the Omega and Bloomsbury. Henderson retrospectively observing that he and Paolozzi had been 'quite long on art and a bit short on craft'.[7]

Much the same could be said of the members of another artists' cooperative venture – Porthia Textile Prints – set up by the sculptor Denis Mitchell in St Ives, Cornwall, in 1957.[8] When interviewed in 2002, Terry Frost – who sometimes assisted Mitchell with the printing – described Porthia Prints as 'just a way of making a bit of extra money' for the artists involved.[9] At least 15 painters and sculptors associated with St Ives took part in the project, amongst them artists as distinguished as Barbara Hepworth, Roger Hilton and Peter Lanyon. Another, already with considerable professional experience of textile design, was the painter and art critic, Patrick Heron, who designed fashion yardage and headsquares in the 1930s and 1940s for his father's company, Cresta Silks. Heron does not, however, appear to have shared his knowledge with others taking part in the project, for Terry Frost recalled, with some amusement, that those

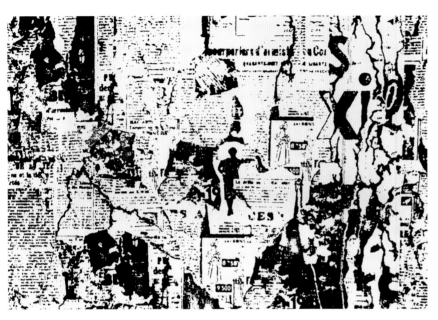

7 Above 'Newsprint', circa 1954. A furnishing textile by Hammer Prints Ltd. A translation of Nigel Henderson's 'Paris Wall' of 1949, a random collage of photographs of advertising hoardings and walls around the city.

8 Opposite Screen-printed tablemat designed by Barbara Hepworth for a series produced by Porthia Prints, St Ives, circa 1957. Porthia Prints, which flourished between 1957 and 1960, was set up by Hepworth's assistant, the sculptor Dennis Mitchell. The series featured designs by most of the main artists resident in Cornwall at that time, including Terry Frost, Roger Hilton and Peter Lanyon.

[6] Victoria Walsh, *Nigel Henderson: Parallel of Life and Art*, 2001, 'The Early Years 1917-1949' pp. 13-14.

[7] Ibid. 'Towards a Conclusion: Hammer Prints' p. 137.

[8] David Buckman, *Dictionary of Artists in Britain since 1945*, 1998, p. 857.

[9] Terry Frost, interview with the author, April 2002.

involved in production had little, if any, understanding of the difference between the inks and methods used for making artists prints and those used for printing textiles; the project's various lines of table mats and domestic linens ran and faded when washed.[10] Porthia Prints continued for three years before closing in 1960.

The painter Louis Le Brocquy, considered by many the outstanding Irish artist of the twentieth century, was one of four painters commissioned by the Dublin-based textile manufacturer John McGuire in 1953, to design an exclusive range of textiles, silk-screened on high quality Irish linen, for the Dublin department store, Brown Thomas of Grafton St. The project may have been influenced by the success of 'Painting into Textiles' held that same year. Besides Le Brocquy, the other painters involved were Nevill Johnson, Patrick Scott and Thurloe Conolly. The resulting fabrics, outstanding amongst them Le Brocquy's 'Megalithic' and 'Flight', had considerable artistic merit and made a distinguished Irish contribution to textile design as an art form. They were subsequently exhibited by the *Société des artistes décorateurs*, at the *Grand Palais* in Paris in May 1954.

Throughout their long careers Le Brocquy and Patrick Scott were also involved with the revival of the art of tapestry, designing for, amongst others, Tabard Frères et Soeurs, Aubusson, and the Edinburgh Tapestry Company. Le Brocquy went to Spain for *The Ambassador* in 1955, where he made drawings and paintings, and co-directed photography with Elsbeth Juda, who worked under the name of Jay. On his return to London, he used these as a basis for designs for the 'Iberian' range of furnishing textiles produced by David Whitehead Ltd in 1956. Two other manufacturers, Seker's Silks and Horrockses, produced fashion textiles from Le Brocquy's Spanish expedition drawings, one of which, 'Furrows', was worn by Princess Margaret on her tour of Africa in 1956.The textiles were promoted in *The Ambassador,*[11] and in 1956 were exhibited, with related drawings and photographs, by Le Brocquy's London gallery, Gimpel Fils.

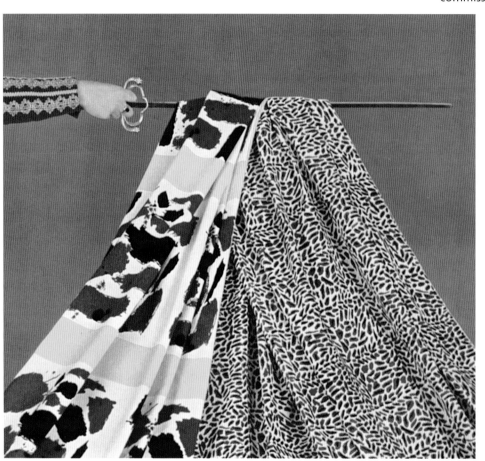

9 Above Le Brocquy travelled to Spain with *The Ambassador* and Elsbeth Juda in 1955. The two printed cottons illustrated here were produced by David Whitehead Ltd for their 'Iberian' range, circa 1956. These and others by Sekers and Horrockses were developed from sketches made on his trip to Spain. The artworks and resultant textiles were exhibited at the London art gallery Gimpel Fils.

10 Opposite Detail of textile designed by Louis Le Brocquy and produced by David Whitehead as part of the 'Iberian' range, circa 1956.

[10] Ibid.

[11] *The Ambassador*, 1956, no. 10, 'Pattern in Contrast', pp. 100-125

11 Opposite 'Barkcloth'
designed by Eduardo
Paolozzi for his own
company, Hammer Prints
Ltd, 1954. The sculptor
Paolozzi in conjunction
with his co-founder,
the photographer
Nigel Henderson,
indiscriminately screen-
printed their idiosyncratic
designs onto wallpapers,
ceramics, table tops and
even ties and scarves.

12 Next spread A screen-printed rayon textile designed
by Eduardo Paolozzi, circa 1953, and produced by
David Whitehead Ltd.

13 Previous page left Taken from *The Ambassador* magazine, a photograph by Jay (Elsbeth Juda) featuring John Tullis's dress design in Paolozzi's fashion fabric for Horrockses.

14 Previous page right Dress designed by John Tullis for Horrockses Fashions, made from a textile designed by Eduardo Paolozzi. The artwork for this textile was one of two by Paolozzi exhibited at 'Painting into Textiles', 1953. Highly publicized at the time, this stunning design was produced in at least two colourways.

15 Opposite 'Foliate Head', designed by John Piper and produced by David Whitehead Ltd in 1954. Piper's original painting for this textile was exhibited in 'Painting into Textiles' in 1953. Foliate Heads were a favoured theme for Piper, who used them in scarf, rug and tapestry design throughout his career.

16 A collage-based abstract
design by Jon Catleugh,
produced by David Whitehead
Ltd. The Lancashire-based
firm produced three textiles
by Catleugh, all of which were
developed from artworks
exhibited at 'Painting into
Textiles', 1953.

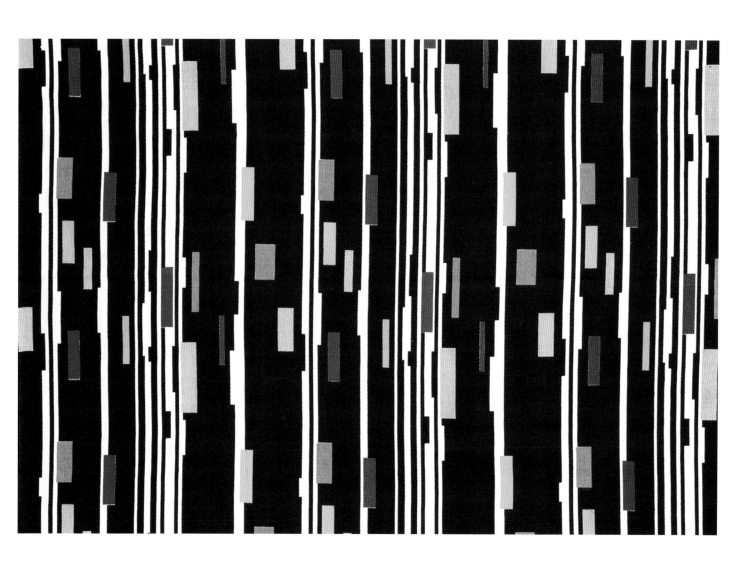

17 A screen-printed rayon textile produced by David Whitehead Ltd, from a collage by Jon Catleugh exhibited at 'Painting into Textiles', 1953.

18 'Blenheim Gates', designed
by John Piper for David
Whitehead Ltd, 1954.

19 'Church Monuments,
Exton' by John Piper, was
screen-printed onto cotton
by David Whitehead Ltd,
circa 1954. Architectural
subjects made up the majority
of textile designs by Piper.

20 'Cyclades', a printed cotton textile by Donald Hamilton Fraser, based on a painting he had exhibited at 'Painting Into Textiles' in 1953, but not issued by David Whitehead until about 1960.

21 'Cockpit', by Martin
Bradley, produced by
Liberty of London in 1957.

22 'Fighting Cocks',
Martin Bradley, dated 1956.

23 'Tampico', designed by
the painter Martin Bradley
for Liberty of London, 1954.

24 'Segment', designed by Michael O'Connell for Heals, circa 1955. Unlike the majority of this artist's work this design is screen-printed. O'Connell had perfected a unique wax-resist batik process for which he became well known, but he did also produce several screen- and block-printed designs for Edinburgh Weavers and Heals.

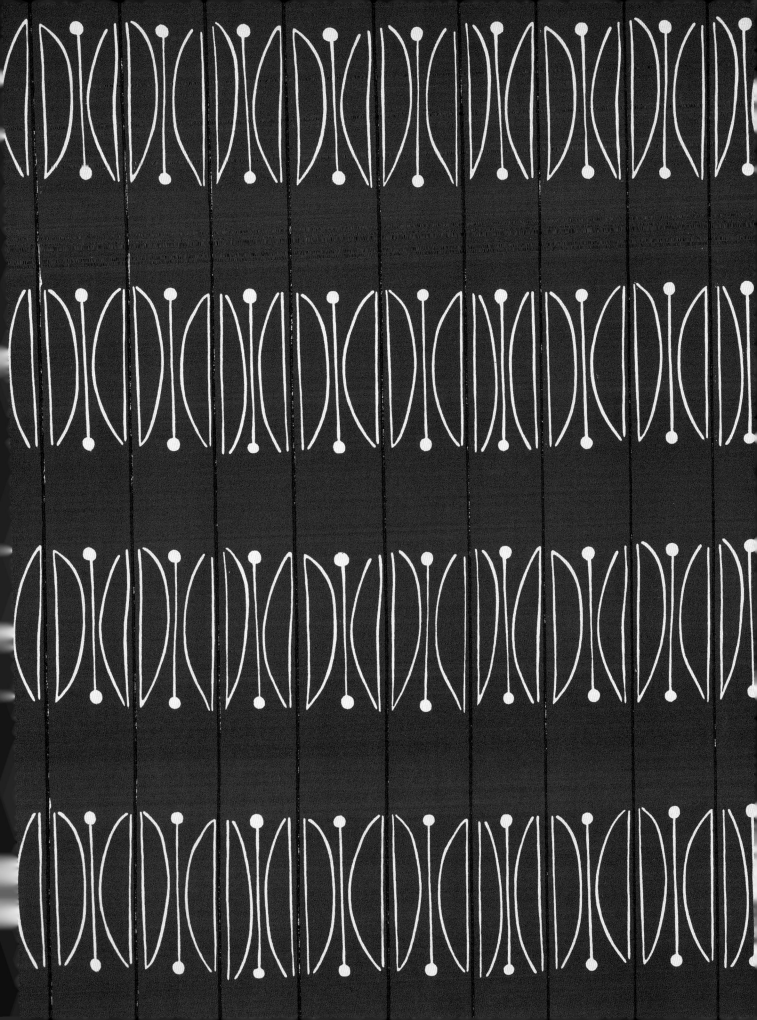

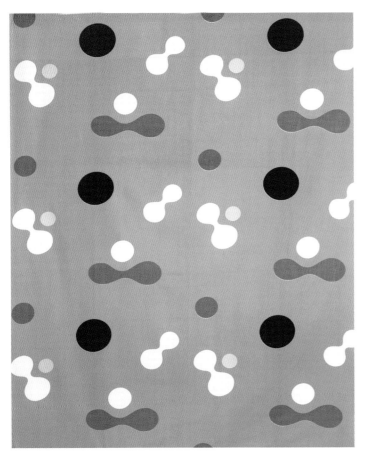

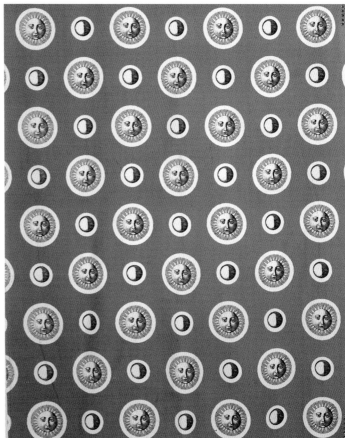

25 Opposite 'Harmony', designed by Paule Vézelay for Heals, 1956. Vézelay created a series of unique, cool, abstract textile designs for Heals over the course of a decade but the relationship was terminated in the early 1960s when Heals felt it could no longer meet Vézelay's increasing fees for designs.

26 Above left 'Modulation' by Paule Vézelay, printed by Heals in 1956.

27 Above right Textile designed by the American sculptor Mitzi Cunliffe, for David Whitehead Ltd, 1955.

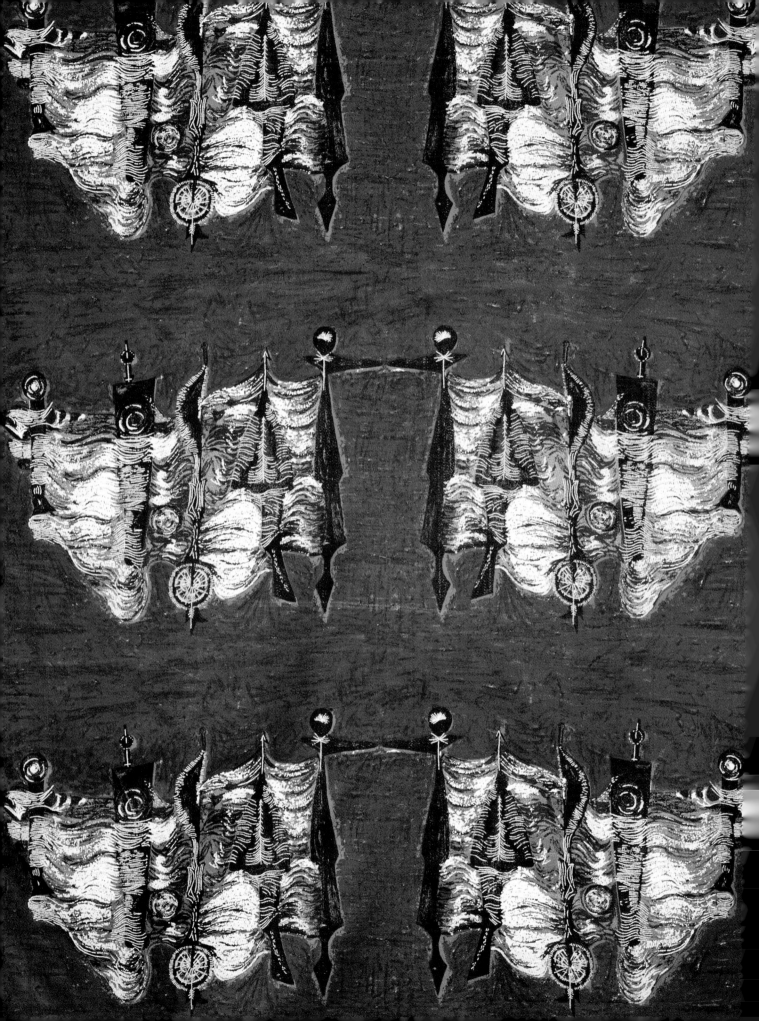

28 Opposite 'Voyagers', a screen-printed, satinised rayon fabric, designed by the painter Gordon Dent and produced by Heals in 1957.

29 Right William Gear, 'Tropic', for Edinburgh Weavers Ltd, circa 1954. One of three desings Morton purchased in 1953 from the 'Painting into Textiles' exhibition.

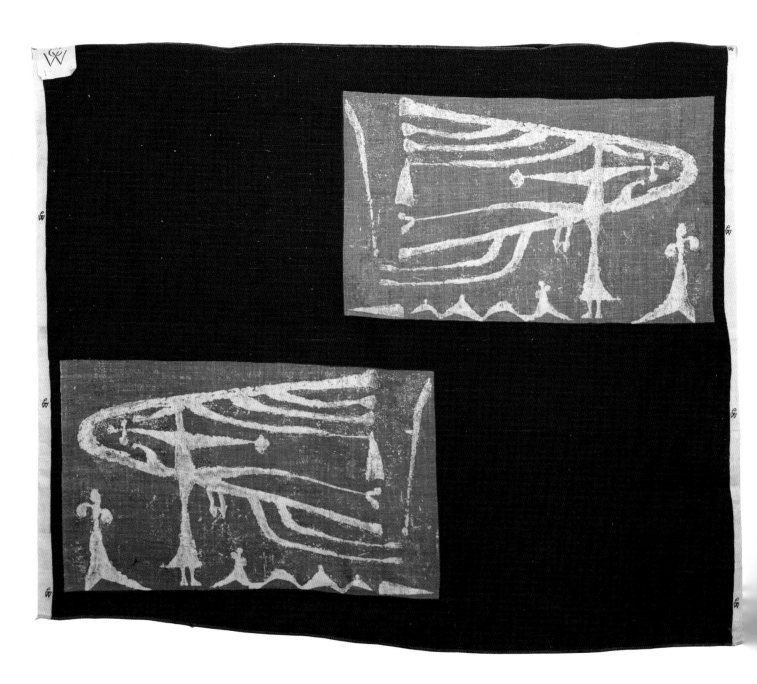

30 Above 'The Grape',
a screen-printed linen,
designed by the sculptor
Geoffrey Clarke for
Edinburgh Weavers, 1956.

31 Opposite 'The Dolmen',
circa 1957, by Geoffrey Clarke,
a screen-printed satinised
cotton, produced by
Edinburgh Weavers.

32 Humphrey Spender's
dramatic collage-based
abstract textile was designed
for Edinburgh Weavers and
produced circa 1960.

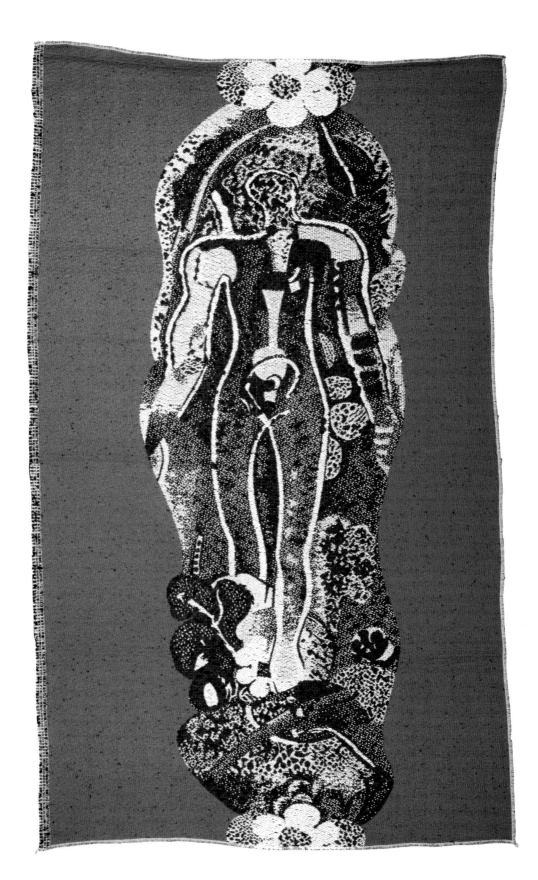

33 Right 'Adam', a woven cotton and rayon furnishing fabric designed by Keith Vaughan for Edinburgh Weavers, 1957.
The fabric won the Design Centre Award for Best Woven Textile, 1958.

34 Opposite 'Matador', a screen-printed satinised cotton by the painter Anthony Harrison for Edinburgh Weavers Ltd, 1958.

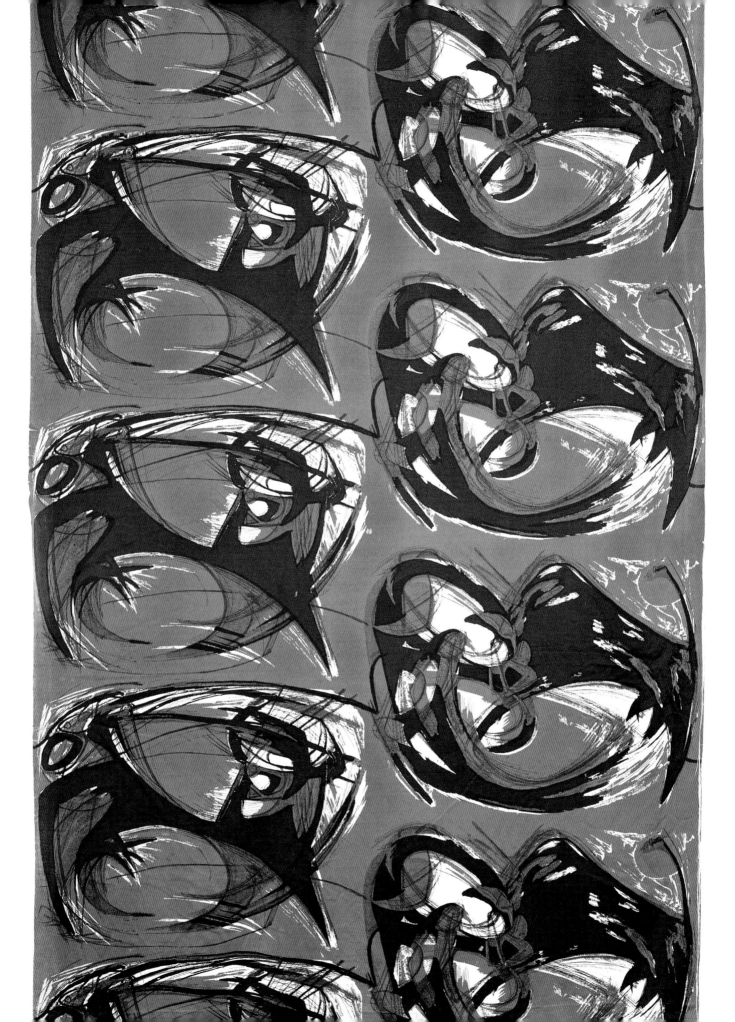

35 Opposite 'Full Measure'
designed by the painter
Kenneth Rowntree for
Edinburgh Weavers, 1957.
Rowntree designed several
textiles for the company
during the mid-to late-1950s.

36 Next spread one 'Flight', designed by Louis Le Brocquy
and hand-printed onto Irish linen by John McGuire Ltd,
Dublin, 1954. This and another design by Le Brocquy for
McGuire, 'Megalithic', were exhibited by the Société des
Artistes Décorateurs at the Grande Palais, Paris, in the
same year.

37 Next spread two 'La Cirque', designed by the Irish
painter Nevill Johnson, and hand screen-printed onto
Irish linen by the Dublin firm of John McGuire, 1954.
Other painters who created designs for McGuire include
Patrick Scott and Thurloe Connolly.

The decade opened with the launch of 'A Fish is a Fish is a Fish…' an influential textile the title of which is a parody of the well-known line from Gertrude Stein's poem 'Sacred Emily'.

America: Ken Scott, 'A Fish is a Fish is a Fish.....'; Associated American Artists, the 'Signature Range'; D B Fuller & Co, 'Modern Masters Prints'; Saul Steinberg for Patterson Fabrics, Piazza Prints, Greef Fabrics

The decade opened with the launch of 'A Fish is a Fish is a Fish...' an influential textile designed by the painter Ken Scott, a protege of Peggy Guggenhiem, for the New York textile company W.B. Quaintence in 1952.(12) It was this textile, the title of which is a parody of the well known line from Gertrude Stein's poem of 1913, 'Sacred Emily, 'A Rose is a Rose is a Rose...', which initiated Scott's Long and successful career as a textile and fashion designer.

In the early 1950s Reeves Lewenthal collaborated with Lowenstein & Sons and Riverdale Fabrics to produce ranges of fashion and furnishing fabrics designed by the artists represented by his gallery, Associated American Artists (AAA). Since the early 1930s, Lewenthal had successfully promoted the work of his artists, by selling their prints through widespread advertising and marketing campaigns to a large and profitable middle class market, but, unlike competitors such as Alan Gruskin of New York's Midtown Gallery, it was some time before he involved AAA in the field of applied art. When he did, it was on the usual Lewenthal scale, with high profile promotions of large collections of furnishing textiles, produced by Riverdale, and ranges of fashion textiles, 'Signature Fabrics', manufactured and marketed by M. Lowenstein & Sons, with the artist or designer's name and the textile's title and date printed on the selvedge. AAA subsequently developed a range of home furnishings with Riverdale using the same designs for a coordinated range of ceramics by Stonelain and wallpapers by United Wallpapers. The commercialization by Lewenthal of his artists' work harks back to similar projects by gallery owners such as Gruskin in the 1940s. After 1957 the advertisements for AAA products cease to appear in magazines such as *American Fabrics*.

By far the most prestigious collaboration in America of artists with the textile industry was that between Fuller Fabrics Inc. and some of the most internationally renowned artists of the twentieth century. The breadth and brilliance of the Fuller project, 'Modern Master Prints', was

38 Right Advertisement for Fuller Fabrics' 'Modern Master Prints', 1955, with swatches of textiles attached. Initially five artists were commissioned for the range and Georges Braque and Paul Klee were added the following year.

39 Opposite 'Carnivale', a fashion fabric from 1954 by the painter Vincent Malta, is one of the many brilliant, eclectic designs from Associated American Artists' 'Signature' range produced by M. Lowenstein from 1952.

12 Illustrated in an advertisement for W B Qaintence, *Interiors*, September 1951.

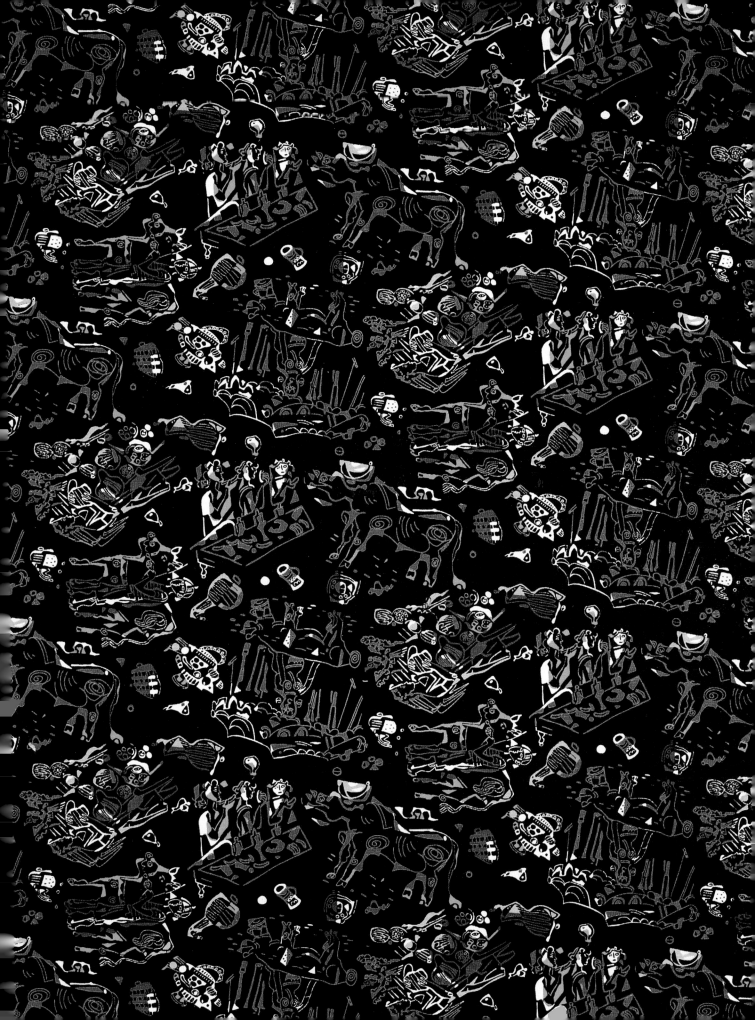

40 'A Fish is a Fish is a Fish',
designed by the painter and
designer Ken Scott and
illustrated in *Interiors*
magazine, September 1951.
Shown here is a border
printed version for dresses
and skirts. It was also printed
as a furnishing textile by
W.B. Quaintence of New York
and was marketed in the
United Kingdom through
Sanderson & Son Ltd.

41 Opposite Dress designed by Claire McCardell for Townleys, using Picasso's 'Fish' print, 1955. Manufactured by Fuller Fabrics, 1955.

42 Above 'Gay Facade'(sic), designed by the Montana-based artist John Hull and illustrated in an article on Associated American Artists' 'Signature' range in *American Fabrics*, 1952.

13 Anon, 'Trying Abstraction on Fabrics', *ARTnews*, November 1955, p. 43.

14 Ibid.

15 Ibid.

16 'Great Art and Fashion Fabrics: the Saga of Dan Fuller and Five Modern Masters', *American Fabrics*, winter 1955, pp. 52-55.

17 'New Fabrics put Modern Art in Fashion', *Life*, November 1955, pp. 140-144.

18 *ARTnews*, November 1955, p. 43.

19 Mendes and Hinchcliffe, *Ascher, Fabric – Art – Fashion*, 1987, p. 27.

equalled only by that in Britain, in the previous decade, of Zika and Lida Ascher. Unlike Dan Fuller however, the Aschers were never able to gain Pablo Picasso's cooperation, and it was the success of Fuller's initial approach to Picasso in 1953, that subsequently ensured his introduction to Joan Miró, Fernand Léger, Marc Chagall and to Raoul Dufy's widow.

The basis of the project was the selection by each artist, in conjunction with Fuller, of motifs taken from the entire gamut of their oeuvre. This in turn initiated two years of painstaking cooperation between each artist and Fuller Fabrics' design and production teams to successfully translate the chosen motifs as textile designs. Each artist's palette was surveyed to pick the final colour range: "with due attention to the limits and special effects of printing dyes; and the special nuances of medium were preserved. The technically difficult process of engraving and printing on cloth required more than a year."[13]

The decision to use roller printing, rather than silk screen, was a sure indicator of the company's intention to produce the textiles on a potentially vast scale, which they planned to sell in the lower price range at between $1.49 and $1.98 a yard.[14] Several leading American fashion designers, Claire McCardell and Wesley Simpson's wife Adele amongst them,[15] created designs using the textiles which were lavishly featured in *American Fabrics*[16] and *Life* magazine.[17] Garment manufacturers throughout the US, such as the distinguished fashion company, Lanz of California, also placed orders, and Fuller Fabrics announced that dresses for the teenage market were to be made up at about $20 a dress.[18] A newspaper advertisement from 1956 for Pomeroy's department store in Reading, Berks County, Pennsylvania, advertised children's 'Modern Masters Print Dresses in Fuller Drip 'n' Dry Fabric, with designs by Picasso and Chagall, for $8.98'.

This was literally art by the yard for the masses, something very close to Picasso's political beliefs, which may well have influenced his decision to take part in the project and to persuade others to do so. He and the other painters involved were some of the most acclaimed artists of the twentieth century, who were neither in need of publicity nor money. Until then Picasso had avoided requests to design textiles,[19] the two exceptions being the design of an inexpensive cotton scarf, given

43a Previous page, inset left Picasso's wife Jacqueline Roque, wearing a blouse made up from one of his textiles for Fuller's, while enjoying 'simple fare at home' with him. Photographed by Edward Quinn and published in Quinn's *Picasso at Work*, 1965.

43b Previous page left A detail of Picasso's textile 'Notes', for Fuller Fabric's 'Modern Master' range, 1955. Leisure or resort ware was the preferred use for the range, much of it aimed at the burgeoning teenage market.

44a Previous page, inset right Picasso and Dan Fuller, President of Fuller Fabrics, photographed in the artists garden comparing Picasso's painting of fighting gamecock with the textile design and the finished fabric, for *American Fabrics*, 'Great Art & Fashion Fabrics; the Saga of Dan Fuller and Five Modern Masters', 1955.

44b Previous page right 'The Rooster' by Picasso for Fuller Fabrics, 1955.

45 Opposite 'Wedding', a furnishing fabric designed by Saul Steinberg and printed by Patterson Fabrics, circa 1950.

20 *ARTnews*, November 1955, p. 43.

21 Victoria and Albert Museum, London, Prints and Drawings Study Room, accession no. E557 – 1966, for wallpaper sample, 1946; cover of *Harper's Bazaar*, March 1947 for image of silk scarf.

22 Harvey M. Smith of Patterson Fabrics, New York, letter to Saul Steinberg, 27 April 1954, Coll. Saul Steinberg Papers, Yale University Library.

away to students and young people at an international peace rally in Berlin in 1951, and the gift that same year of a design for a limited edition silk scarf sold to raise funds for the Institute of Contemporary Arts in London.

The Fuller project culminated in 60 designs for fashion and furnishing fabrics. Those for fashion were launched at an exhibition at the Brooklyn Museum, New York, in October 1955, featuring the sources and finished fabrics, as well as a colour film documentary of the artists at work in their studios.[20] The range of furnishing textiles introduced the following year by the company's Decorama Division was a more exclusive affair, and was only available to the public through interior decorators. Later that year, designs derived from the work of two other major twentieth-century artists, Georges Braque and the then long deceased Paul Klee, were added to the ranges, but by 1957 the project had run its course.

Another artist who had the occasional brush with textile design in the 1950s was the satirical cartoonist, graphic designer and illustrator, Saul Steinberg, whose cover designs and cartoons for The *New Yorker* were the epitome of sophisticated cool in the post-war era. His work set the benchmark in the 1940s and 1950s for what became a distinctive New York school of Illustration and graphic design, whose leading exponents were Andy Warhol and John Rombola.

In 1946, capitalizing on the popularity and novelty of Steinberg's work, a small New York based company, Piazza Prints, collaborated with him in adapting a number of his witty designs to wallpapers and textiles;[21] 'Views of Paris' for example was used for both a scarf and a wallpaper. From 1947 Patterson Fabrics, a subsidiary of Piazza Prints, also produced furnishing textiles with Steinberg's designs, including 'Views of Paris'. For over seven years they made a substantial investment producing and promoting Steinberg's textiles, which – believing themselves his sole manufacturer, distributor and agent – they thought were exclusive to themselves.

However, this was not the case, as the story laid out in a letter to Steinberg from an executive of Patterson's, Harvey M. Smith, illustrates.[22] This letter, and other related correspondence in the Steinberg papers, provide a remarkable insight into the pitfalls and problems encountered by an artist working in the American textile industry in the early 1950s, as well as the level of corporate investment and the commitment involved in the development and promotion of textile ranges.

46 'Les Gendarmes',
illustrated in *Interiors*, 1954.
Steinberg's design for Greef
was produced as textile and
wallpaper.

[23] 'Les Gendarmes', illustrated
in *Interiors*, February 1954, p. 79.

In the letter, dated 27 April 1954, Smith invites Steinberg to have lunch at the company's New York offices with himself and Mr Piazza, in order to have 'a serious discussion in relation to the number and kind of firms which offer your designs to decorators'. The root of the problem for Patterson was the discovery that Steinberg had misled them over the type of firm to whom he had recently sold textile designs. This company had turned out to be 'a direct competitor dealing with the exact same customers in precisely the same neighborhoods. As you know, their New York office is scarcely half a block from our New York office'.

Smith continues with what he saw as further duplicity on Steinberg's part with regard to the designs he had sold to this competitor. He writes he had been in error about the designs being different from the type they had developed:

"After experimenting with the first two types we finally arrived at the third type which is by far the most desirable from the decorators stand point. It is in this third type that your designs for this other firm fall, a type which took your work and our expense and effort and experimentation five years to reach."

The letter then comes to what must have been an extremely embarrassing, even humiliating, experience for the company.

"While recently away on my vacation I was asked by my Office if we had a new Steinberg pattern of policemen, and since returning I have learned from an *Interiors* that it is a design done for the other house."

Apparently, Patterson's had been receiving requests from decorators for designs that, although by Steinberg, were not produced by them. Smith continues:

"It is obvious that the decorators are not able to see any difference between the designs we offer and the designs offered by our competitor, and frankly, neither can I. During the past year we have had quite a large number of requests oral and written for patterns of yours, which we do not have. This merely indicates that the decorating trade expects to find your work at our premises, and that even if they have seen the other design they still frequently come to us for it … This is a bad situation and one for which I know of no parallel."

By working for a number of companies, Smith admits, Steinberg will, in the short term, make more money, but his work will quickly pall and become unfashionable. Unlike Patterson, who were only interested in establishing their designers work for the long haul, Smith writes:

"This [other] firm was only interested in your work after it was slowly and carefully introduced and established in the decorating field. I do not believe they would have thought of you had we not already done this. Their policy is one of changing stylists every few years. Apparently they want things that will show immediate results regardless of other considerations … We are after seven years due slightly more consideration than is being shown."

The rival company was Greef, a leading 'high-end' textile manufacturer, and the textile depicting policemen, which became the final straw for Smith, was Steinberg's 'Les Gendarmes'[23] (Plate 47).

47 **Previous spread** 'Tin Horn Holiday', a border print on cotton by Saul Steinberg, circa 1952. A tour de force of Steinberg imagery, this design draws on his favourite themes of weekend cowboys and gas-guzzling automobiles, complete with palm trees as lamp posts, decked with ornamental ironwork and hung with fancy shades.

Although, in April 1954, Smith had only recently become aware of Steinberg's relationship with Greef, a letter from the company's President, Theodore Greef, to Steinberg, dated 1 July 1952, already concerns a mutual 'project' to which he looks forward with 'real pleasure'. In the letter Greef details his company's proposed financial arrangements with Steinberg, particularly the various types of royalties they paid to 'those few artists' who had such agreements, and how they intended bringing out a range of his designs by the end of November 1952.[24]

Apparently unknown to either Greef or Patterson, was Steinberg's even earlier negotiation with another prestigious American textile company, Stehli & Co. Inc. In a letter dated 22 May 1950, the company's advertising director, Henry Bonner, reported back to Steinberg Mr. Stehli's thoughts on the artist's suggested fees for designs and royalties. He wrote, that to 'guarantee five thousand dollars or more' for ten designs 'would be out of the question. Mr. Stehli however said he would be perfectly willing to guarantee one thousand dollars ($1000) for ten (10) sketches or one hundred dollars ($100) a sketch, plus five cents ($.05) a yard, which seems to me extremely fair.'[25]

These negotiations do not appear to have gone any further, and there is no subsequent evidence of Steinberg designing for Stehli. The two things that become apparent in these various surreptitious negotiations are Steinberg's concern with money, and a rather short-sighted willingness to exploit situations to his immediate benefit. However, in fairness to him, he was only able to play these companies against each other because of the paranoid secrecy they worked in, which stemmed from their extreme competitiveness and the concomitant fear of industrial espionage damaging their high financial investment. Although seemingly cavalier in his attitude towards the various textile companies he was commissioned by, he was, apparently, alert to any infringement of his copyright, which he was quick to defend; in the process gaining a reputation for being somewhat litigious.

american fabrics

STEINBERG

Vol. 13

In Harvey Smith's letter, he also recalled that Steinberg had previously raised with him the matter of his designing for other textile companies,

"During the past seven years we have spoken briefly on several occasions about your designing for other textile houses. Generally these houses were dress goods firms or large downtown (4th Avenue and lower) convertors. There could be no objection on my part as regards either of these types of houses; that is, there could be no objection on the basis that their sales would conflict with our sales. There remained the fact, regardless of whether you or I objected to it, that the inclusion of your designs in their collections would almost certainly cheapen your name, and hasten the time when the public would be tired of your designs."

Yet, despite Smith's somewhat self-interested advice, it appears Steinberg designed for at least one dress goods firm. The correspondence he received from textile manufacturers show him as much concerned with quantity as quality, for, as well as an upfront fee, royalties were always central to his contractual agreements, rather than, as with many designers, the outright sale of a design. The potentially enormous yardage sales of a successful fashion fabric and the resulting royalties would have proved irresistible to him.

A number of cotton border prints with typically witty and gently satirical 'Steinbergian' designs, suitable for summer dresses and skirts, are known. However, unlike the sensitive, subtly nuanced and finely detailed hand silk screen printing of his exclusive textiles by Patterson, the drawing of these has been simplified and broadened to suit both the requirements of the roller-printing process – then the principal printing method for large scale mass production – and the design of textiles suitable for inexpensive cotton garments intended for the popular market. From Picasso's designs for Fuller through to those of the present day, few, if any, mass-produced textiles result directly from an artist's hand. The vast majority is a collaboration – or compromise – between a company's design team and the artist concerned, and Steinberg would have been no exception.

These border prints have complex and sophisticated narratives: 'Tin Horn Holiday', for example, is a clever send-up of a Palm Springs dude vacation venue; depicting a typical, witty Steinbergian concept of the modern world destroying the old Wild West; except that the Wild West is already long gone; the cowboys are caricatures of themselves acting out a hold-up in a modern desert resort. In another design, a rather woozy group of women and a man touch ground after a roller coaster ride in a highly decorative, Coney Island-type fun fair. Other designs are gentle satires on the typical

destinations of the growing post-war vogue for foreign travel, and are probably a separate series to those featuring American holiday resorts.

The artist and designer John Rombola, who succeeded Steinberg at Piazza Prints in 1956, was well aware, as a young man, of these border prints. He still recalls, with some amusement, seeing women wearing 'those skirts with Steinberg's designs on the New York Subway in the early 1950s.' The skirts were apparently very popular and Rombola estimates the fabric sales would have generated considerable royalties.[26]

There is, tantalizingly, no record of the outcome of Smith and Piazza's proposed lunch with Steinberg in 1954, or if it even took place. Steinberg's involvement with the textile industry seems to have ended by 1956, after which royalty payments from Patterson Fabrics, Piazza Prints and Greef cease to appear in Steinberg's deposit books, an indication that these companies had by then stopped producing and marketing his designs.

48 Opposite Cover of *American Fabrics* Spring 1950, using Steinberg's 'Trains' textile for Patterson Fabrics. Like many of his designs this fabric was also available as a wallpaper printed by Piazza Prints.

[24] Theodore Greef, letter to Saul Steinberg, 1 July 1952, Coll. Saul Steinberg Papers, Yale University Library.

[25] Henry Bonner, Advertising Director, Stehli & Co. Inc., letter to Saul Steinberg, 22 May 1950, Coll. Saul Steinberg Papers, Yale University Library.

[26] John Rombola, interview with author, February 2011.

49 **Previous spread** 'Paddington Station' by Saul Steinberg, circa 1952, one of a series of border prints on regulated cotton intended for use as skirts and dresses.

50 **Below** A Steinberg border print depicting the interior of an opera house, circa 1952.

51 Previous spread Steinberg's witty depiction of a Coney Island type roller coaster ride at a funfair, produced on cotton as a border print for skirts and dresses. The three women, two in 'flyaway butterfly' sunglasses, are a vivid pink, presumably the effect of sunbathing, while their male companion, following the joys of the roller coaster ride, is a fetching shade of green.

52 Below Steinberg used a North African town as the theme for this cotton border print. He visited North Africa whilst serving in the Second World War and had published closely related drawings in his first book, *All in Line*, 1945, and in *The New Yorker*.

53 Next spread 'Savage Parade', a textile designed by Fernand Léger for Fuller Fabrics, 1955.

54 Next spread, inset bottom Dan Fuller with Leger in the artist's studio examining examples of his textiles 'Acrobats' and 'Savage Parade'.

55 Next spread two 'Structures' a furnishing fabric designed by Fernard Léger and printed as part of the Fuller Fabrics 'Decorama' range, 1956.

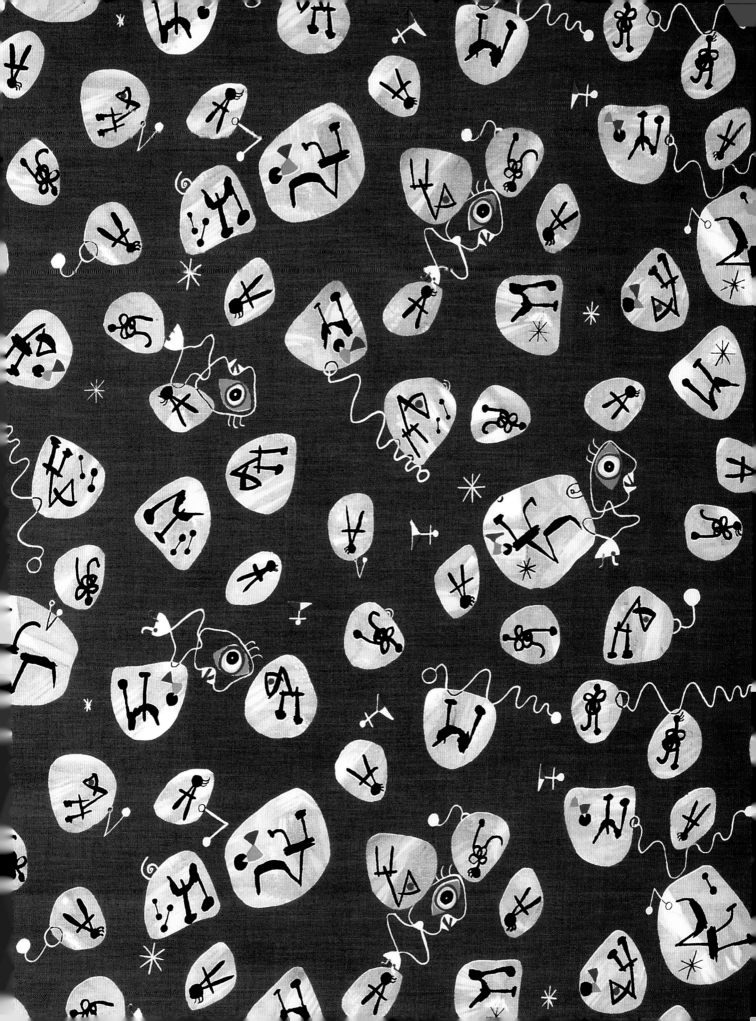

56 Previous spread one 'Femme Écoutant', designed by Joan Miró for Fuller Fabrics, 1955. Miró's aesthetic concepts lent themselves well to fabric design making them some of the most successful in the 'Modern Masters' range.

57 and 57a Previous spread two Joan Miró, 'Farmer's Dinner' printed cotton dress fabric manufactured by Fuller Fabrics, 1955. Inset with dress made from Miró's 'Farmer's Dinner'.

58 Below Dan Fuller and Joan Miro looking at the artist's textiles 'Dancing Figures' and 'Femme Ecoutant'.

59 Opposite 'Dancing Figures', by Joan Miró, 1955, is one of sixty designs produced by Fuller Fabrics under the 'Modern Masters' label.

60 Previous spread one Raoul Dufy's 'Les Maronniers' textile for Fuller Fabrics, produced posthumously in 1955. All of the Dufy designs for the 'Modern Masters' range used classic Dufy subject matter such as seascapes, horse racing and Parisian scenes.

61 Previous spread two 'Orchestra', this printed cotton produced by Fuller Fabrics circa 1955 from a Raoul Dufy design, draws on the many dynamic pen and ink studies from the artist's work of the early 1940s.

62 Opposite 'Belle Fleurs', furnishing fabric designed by Chagall and produced under the Decorama label for Fuller Fabrics, circa 1956. This is one of the 'Modern Master' drapery fabrics included in the Museum of Modern Art's 'Textiles USA' in 1956.

63 Previous page left Marc Chagall, 'A l'Ombre des Reves', a 'Modern Master' fabric designed by Chagall for Fuller Fabrics. A contemporary magazine advertisement for the range stated that, 'the fantasy of Chagall's enchantment with remembered childhood is captured for fashion.'

64 Previous page right 'Morning Mystery', another of Chagall's dress fabrics for Fuller Fabrics.

65 Opposite A screen-printed furnishing fabric, circa 1956, designed by Georges Braque.

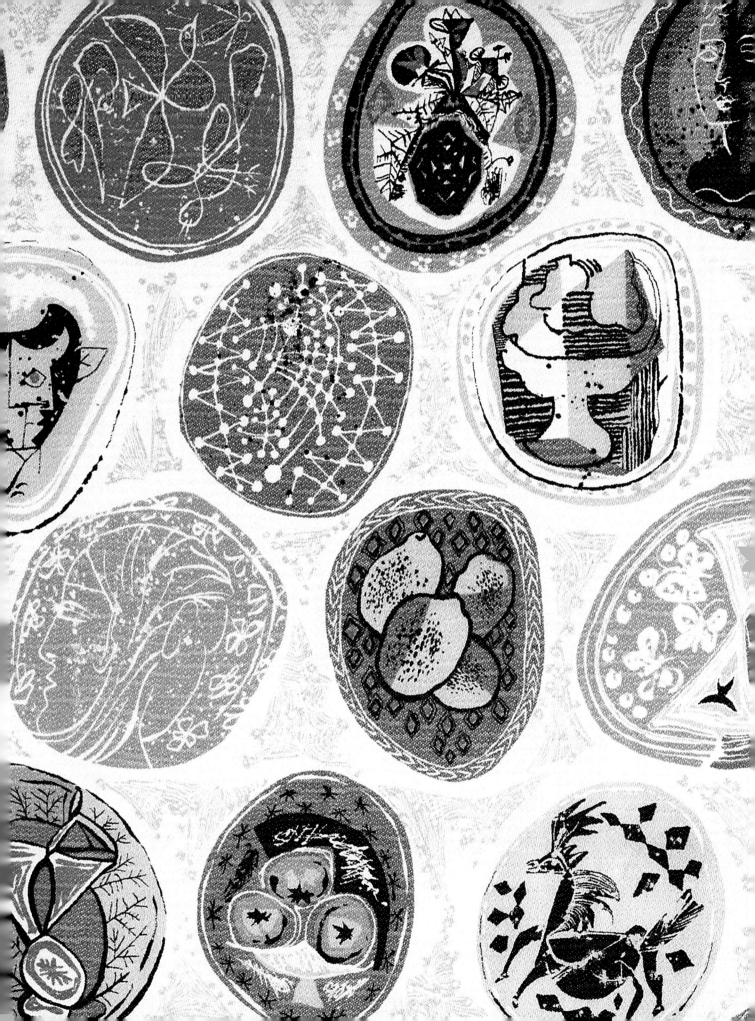

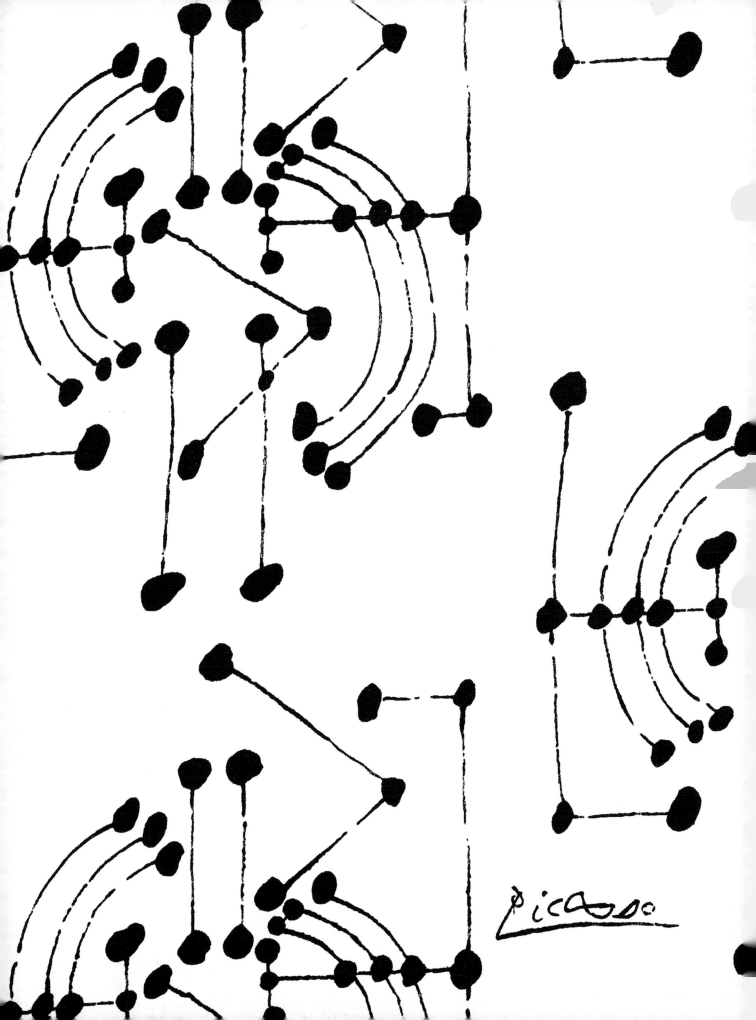

Paradoxically, although a high point in the ascendancy of the Modern Movement, which had dominated western art, architecture and design for more than half of the twentieth century, the 1960s is more usually associated with Pop culture. Pop was essentially an Anglo-American phenomenon and it was in Britain and America that the Pop aesthetic was introduced into textile design by artist-designers such as Andy Warhol and Zandra Rhodes.

THE 1960S

The 1960s: Britain. Sanderson and John Piper; Edinburgh Weavers; Hull Traders; David Whitehead's 'Living Art' collection; Zandra Rhodes and Pop; Liberty and Delaunay

In the aftermath of the destruction caused by the Second World War, a building boom took place in Britain and many of the new public buildings – from schools, universities and hospitals, to corporate headquarters, civic centres and hotels – required furnishing with suitably prestigious furniture, floor coverings and, of course, textiles. The large impressive spaces of the Modernist interiors that the textiles were commissioned for demanded an increasingly monumental scale and grandeur. This situation culminated in 1960 with 'Avon', a textile designed by the painter Cecil Collins, and commissioned by the Ministry of Works from Edinburgh Weavers for the new conference hall of the British Embassy in Washington DC, the grandiose scale of which necessitated a textile with a pattern repeat of some fifteen feet.

In 1959 the distinguished British textile and wallpaper manufacturer Arthur Sanderson and Sons Ltd commissioned five textiles from the painter John Piper for its centenary celebrations the following year. Piper derived the subject matter for them from a wide spectrum of his work, which included designs for stained glass windows for the chapel of Oundle School, Northamptonshire, reinterpreted as the textile 'Arundel', and a study of the Santa Maria della Salute Church, which he had executed in Venice in 1959. He based the designs of the three other textiles in the commission – 'Stones of Bath', 'Northern Cathedral' and 'The Glyders' – on studies of British land- and townscapes.

The various elements contributing to the drama of Piper's textiles were not uncommon in textiles designed by British artists in the early 1960s: typically carried out on an extremely large scale with, frequently, a single image covering the entire width of the fabric. This monumental conception, usually combined with an uncompromising painterly style, drew on a wide diversity of subject matter: from the semi-abstract work of William Scott, Alan Reynolds and Trevor Coleman, to the abstraction of the Situationists such as Harold Cohen and John Plumb. Other artists who contributed to this rich melange were the painters of the Swedish based 'Marstrand Designers': Maj Nilsson, Lisa Grönwall and Cliff Holden, co-founder with David Bomberg

A
CENTURY OF
SANDERSON
1860 - 1960

The jacket design
is reproduced from a sketch by
JOHN PIPER
for the great panel of stained
glass which will greet visitors
in the new Sanderson headquarters
in Berners Street, London.

1 Above Cover to the publication *A Century of Sanderson 1860-1960*, taken from the design, by John Piper, for a stained glass panel executed in 1960 by Patrick Reyntiens for Sanderson's new headquarters, Berners St., London.

2 Opposite 'Arundel', designed by John Piper, one of five designs the artist created for the Sanderson centenary celebrations, 1960. Each of the designs was screen-printed on Sanderlin: a cotton fabric with a permanent glaze finish, developed at Sanderson's Uxbridge Print Works.

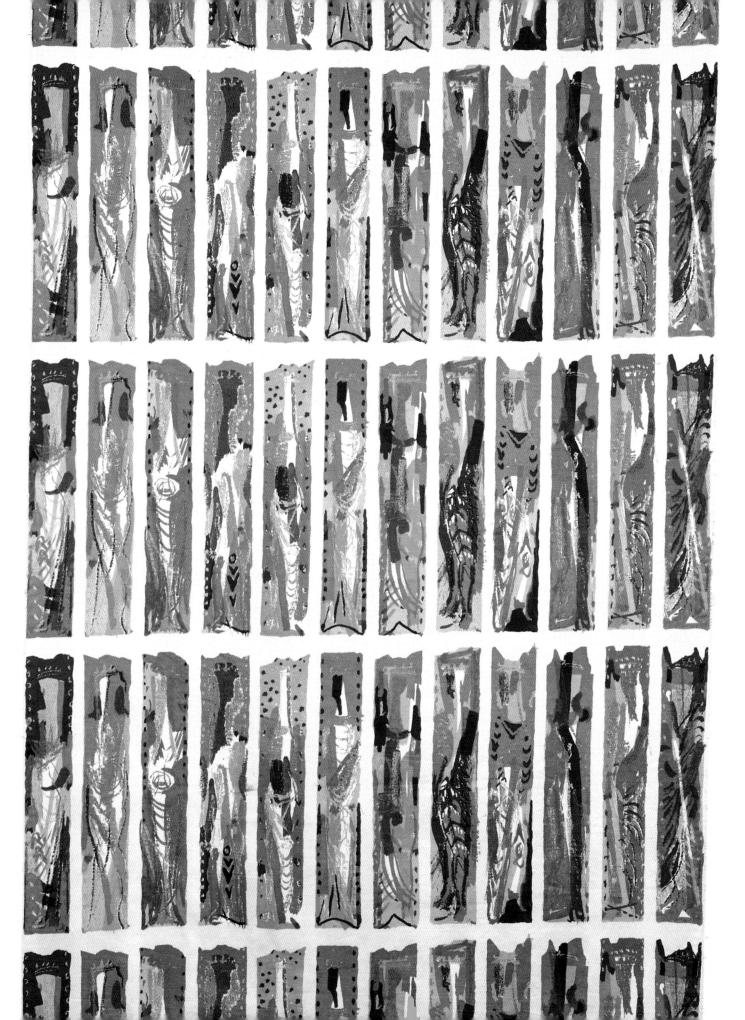

3 **Previous page left** 'Northern Cathedral', commissioned from John Piper in 1959 for the Sanderson centenary, and issued in 1962.

4 **Previous page right** 'Chiesa De La Salute', one of the Sanderson centenary textiles designed by Piper in 1959, and issued in 1960.

5 **Below** A 1962 Edinburgh Weavers advertisement illustrating Joe Tilson's 'Bocca'.

6 **Opposite** 'Warriors', a jacquard-woven furnishing fabric, designed by the sculptor Elisabeth Frink and produced by Edinburgh Weavers, 1960.

in 1946 of the Borough Group. The sculptors Marino Marini and Elisabeth Frink, and the godfather of Op Art, Victor Vasarely, also made significant contributions to this artistic monumentalism in British textile design.

Central to this phenomenon was Edinburgh Weavers, although the company did not long survive the death of its influential director Alastair Morton in 1963. Another eminent manufacturer was Heal Fabrics, which successfully commissioned designs from avant-garde artists such as Plumb and Cohen. Hull Traders Ltd also produced textiles designed by artists throughout the 1960s, amongst them the painters Trevor Coleman and Dorothy Carr; father and son, Ivon and John Hitchens and, in 1967, Richard Allen, a leading proponent of Op Art, who designed two remarkable textiles, Ziminy 1 & 2, for the company. David Whitehead Ltd remained steadfast in its commitment to producing artist designed textiles, continuing to flourish until the end of the decade, when, shortly after the launch of its final artists' collection, 'Living Art', the company was taken over by Lonrho in 1970.

Although many textiles designed by artists in Britain in the 1960s were magnificent works of art, they were far removed from the everyday lives of most people. This was equally true of much else of the Modern Movement's agenda, from which many people, particularly the young, were increasingly alienated, instead becoming more involved with the easily accessible and attractive alternative of Pop culture.

The leading designer of Pop textiles in Britain was Zandra Rhodes, whose work in the 1960s was a dazzling fusion of textile and fashion design with fine art. Rhodes's most successful design was the furnishing fabric 'Top Brass', brought by Heal Fabrics from her diploma show at the Royal College of Art in 1964. However, after leaving the Royal College, her extreme Pop influenced fashion textiles, which she hand silk screen-printed in her studio, proved too difficult for most in the fashion industry to use. Rather than compromise her work, her solution, similar to that of Sonia Delaunay some fifty years earlier, was to design her own fashion collections, which like those of Stepanova and Popova, she conceived in a unity of fashion and textile design and the human form, to create a total work of art.

EDINBURGH WEAVERS
102 MOUNT ST
LONDON W1

≪ BOCCA ≫ A LINEN PRINT DESIGNED BY JO TILSON

7 In this design for David Whitehead, issued around 1960, Piper drew inspiration from figures carved on Cretan Sealstones of the Minoan era, which he had sketched at the British Museum in the 1950s.

8 **Left** Possibly as a response to the Sanderson-Piper collaboration, David Whitehead issued John Piper's 'Cotswold' in 1960.

9 **Opposite** 'Fawley' designed by Piper for David Whitehead, early 1960s, and produced as a screen-printed satinised cotton. The Pipers lived in Fawley Bottom Farmhouse, near Henley, Oxfordshire, from the mid-1930s.

10 Robert Tierney, 'Montrose'
circa 1960, for F W Grafton Ltd.

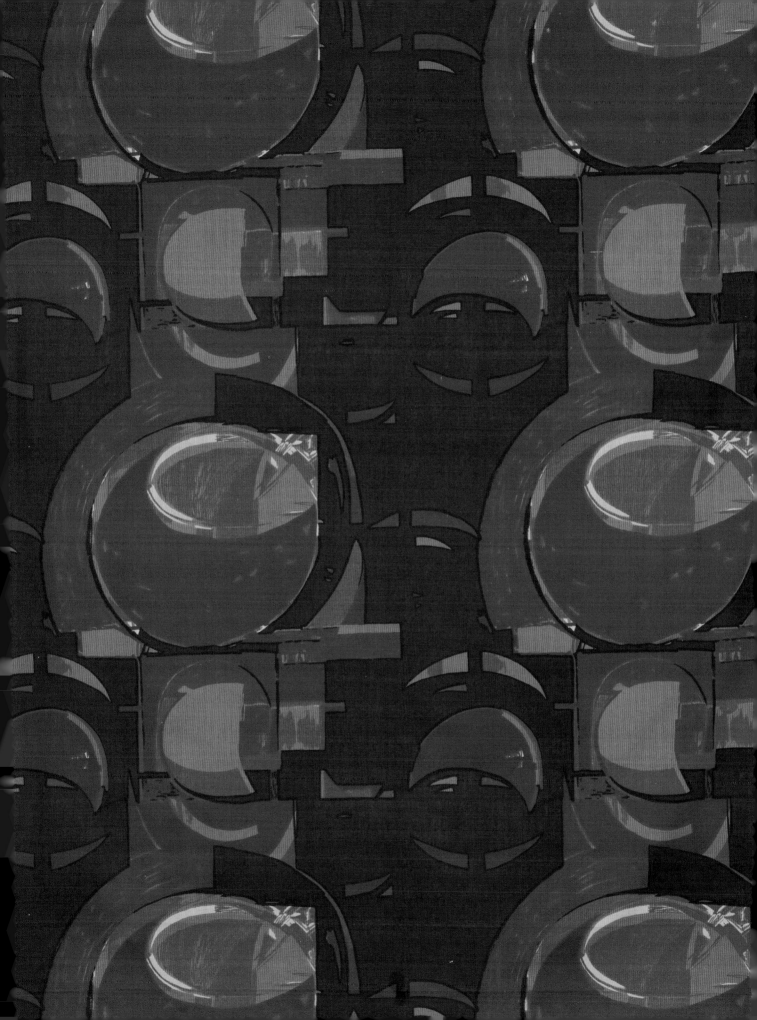

11 Previous page left Harold Cohen, 'Vineyard', screen-printed cotton, designed circa 1959, for Heal Fabrics. Cohen and John Plumb were both members of the Situation Group, established after the successful exhibition of their very large, abstract paintings, 'Situation' at the RBA Galleries in 1960.

12 Previous page right Harold Cohen 'Rough Cast', designed circa 1959 for Heal Fabrics.

13 Opposite John Plumb's 'Chiricahua', for Heal Fabrics, circa 1963.

14 Left 'Fall', designed by Cliff Holden for Heal Fabrics, 1960. Holden, Grönwall and Nilsson, were known collectively as the 'Marstrand Designers'.

15 Centre 'Chartwell' designed by Lisa Grönwall for David Whitehead Ltd, 1959.

16 Right 'Haddon', Maj Nilsson's design for screen-printed cotton, produced by David Whitehead Ltd, 1959.

17 **Previous page left** Victor Vasarely, 'Kernoo', printed cotton furnishing fabric for Edinburgh Weavers Ltd, 1962.

18 **Previous page right** Vasarely's monumental 'Oeta', a jacquard-woven furnishing fabric produced by Edinburgh Weavers, 1962, is based on a series of paintings of the same name, dating from between 1956-1957.

19 **Left** Marino Marini's jacquard-woven furnishing fabric 'Cavallo', issued by Edinburgh Weavers, 1959. The design was produced in cotton for general sale but this version was woven for the Morton family's own use in silk.

20 **Opposite** 'Bird Rose', screen-printed cotton textile by Dennis Hawkins, produced by Edinburgh Weavers, 1963.

21 Alan Reynolds' design, 'Weald', produced by Edinburgh Weavers Ltd, 1959. Along with a number of other Edinburgh Weavers designs, including Frink's 'Warriors' and Marini's 'Cavallo', this was exhibited at 'Modern Art in Textile Design', Whitworth Art Gallery, Manchester, 1962.

22 'Crystalline Image'. A
Jacquard woven cotton and
rayon fabric, translated from
a painting by Reynolds in
1958, and included in the
Edinburgh Weavers
catalogue, Autumn 1961.

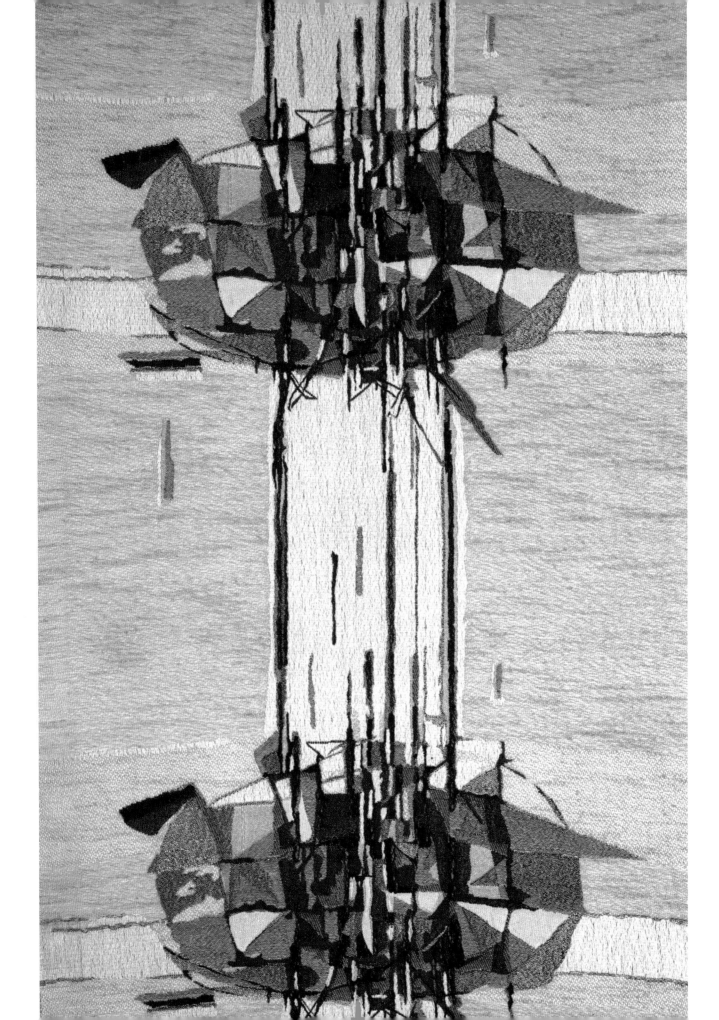

23 The screen-printed cotton fabric, 'Legend', is a translation of Alan Reynolds' painting 'Structure with Black Ovoid', purchased by Alistair Morton from the Redfern Gallery, London, in September 1962. The resulting textile was produced by Edinburgh Weavers in around 1963-4 and won a Design Centre Award in 1965.

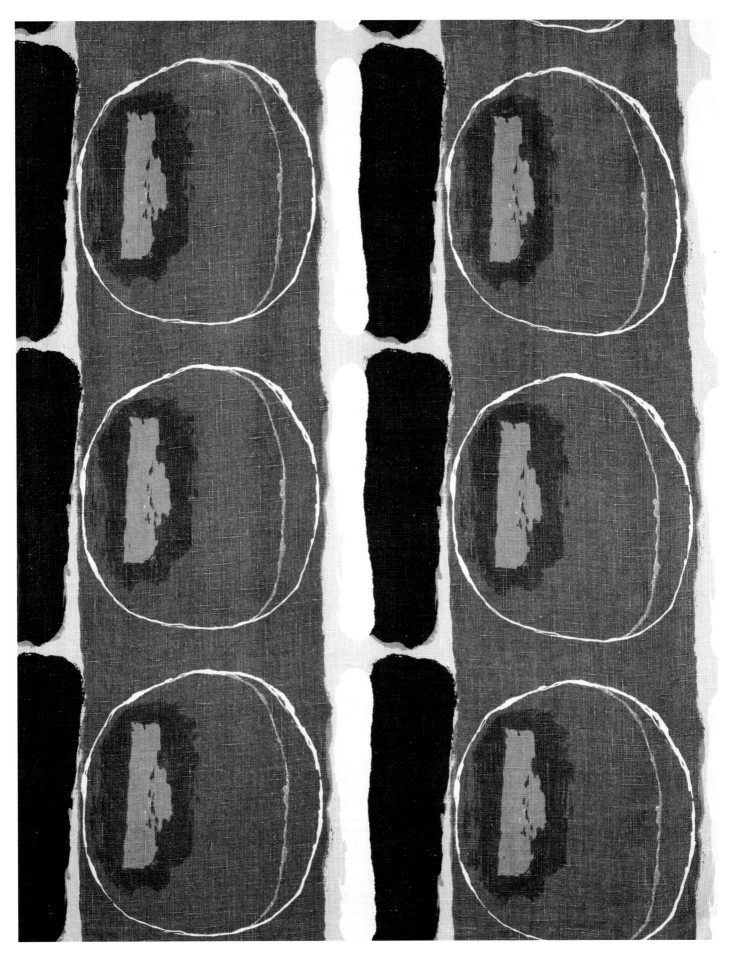

24 Previous page left 'Skara Brae' a printed cotton tweed furnishing fabric designed by William Scott and produced by Edinburgh Weavers, 1958. The design is a translation of Scott's painting of the neolithic settlement on the west coast of Orkney, Scotland.

25 Previous page right 'Whithorn', by William Scott, was commissioned by the architect Eugene Rosenberg, of Yorke, Rosenberg and Mardall, as an integral component of the interiors of the Altnagelvin Hospital, Londonderry, Northern Ireland. Rosenberg strongly believed in integrating art within architectural settings, a subject on which he subsequently wrote in his book of 1992, *Art in Architecture in Great Britain since 1945*. 'Whithorn' was produced by Edinburgh Weavers as a screen printed linen in 1961, and was subsequently available to the public.

26 Opposite 'Totem', screen-printed cotton designed by the South African painter, Trevor Coleman, for Hull Traders Ltd, 1963.

27 'Summer Flowers',
an amalgamation of two
flower paintings by father
and son, Ivon and John
Hitchens, for Hull Traders,
was one of the company's
earliest commissions and
attracted considerable
attention when it was
eventually launched in 1961.

28 'Ziminy One', and its colour inverse, 'Ziminy Two' were designed by the noted Op Art artist Richard Allen for Hull Traders in 1967.

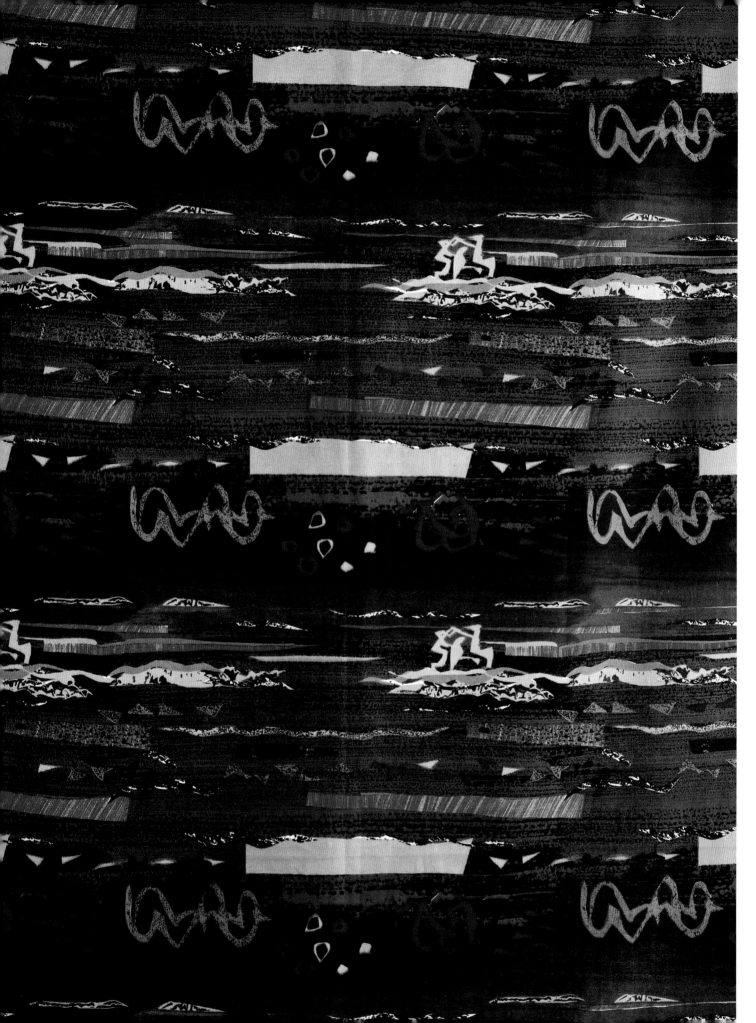

29 **Previous page left** 'Brittany', by John Piper, is an
interpretation of gouache and cut marbled paper collages,
such as 'Brittany Beach' and 'La Pointe du Château',
which were carried out on an excursion to Brittany in 1960.
The resulting images were used to create this textile for
David Whitehead's 'Living Art' collection, launched in 1969.

30 **Previous page right** Another design from the David
Whitehead 'Living Art' collection is Jack Packenham's
'Poole', designed in 1968, and produced as a screen-
printed cotton.

31 **Below left** 'Technicus'
by Merrick Hansel for David
Whitehead's 'Living Art'
collection, launched in 1969.

32 **Below right** 'Sun God'
by Pádraig Macmiadhacháin
for David Whitehead's
'Living Art' collection, 1969.

33 **Opposite** 'Clare',
by George Campbell
for David Whitehead's
'Living Art' collection, 1969.
Campbell was one of a
number of Irish painters
represented in what
transpired to be Whitehead's
last artist designed textile
project.

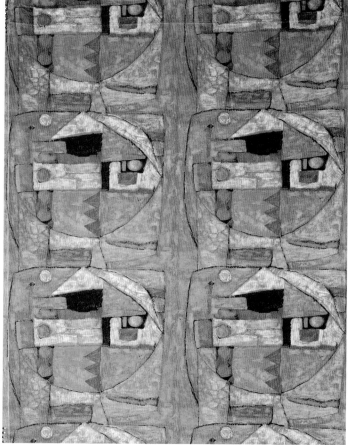

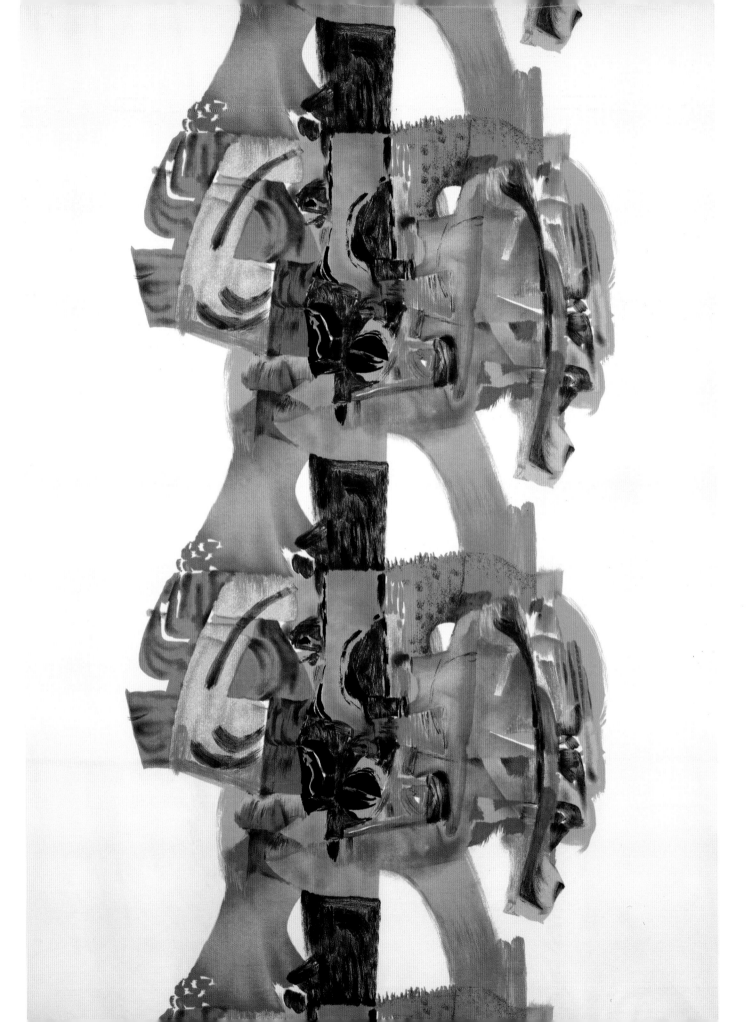

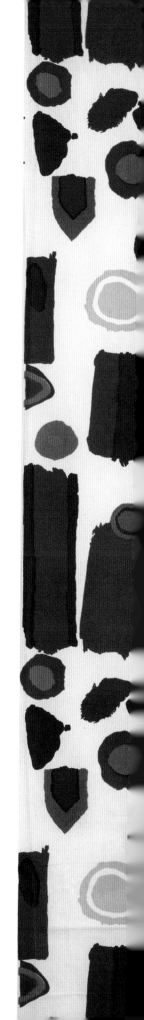

34 Zandra Rhodes textile 'Medals' was displayed in her diploma shows at the Royal College of Art in 1964. Her original inspiration was David Hockney's painting of 1961, 'A Grand Procession of Dignitaries painted in Semi-Egyptian Style'. Heal Fabrics brought the design from Rhodes that year and produced it as a screen-printed furnishing cotton, 'Top Brass'.

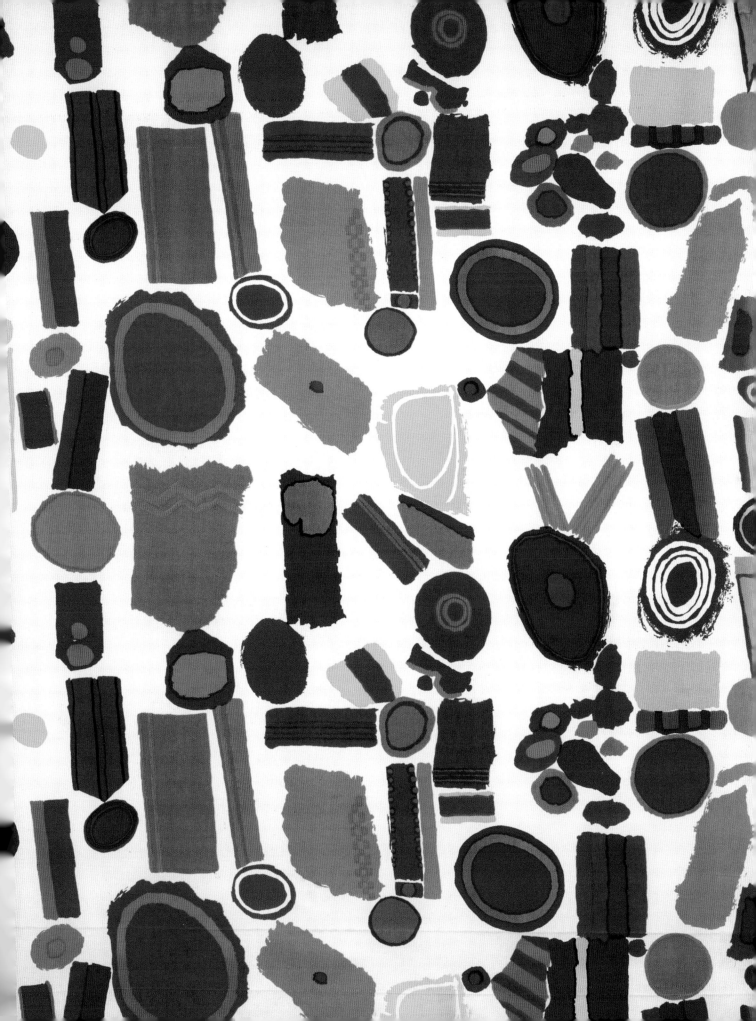

35 Previous spread This Rhodes furnishing textile combined
her 'Mr Man' and 'All Over Neon' patterns and was printed
by her around 1968.

36 Opposite 'Lipstick' a screen-
printed silk crêpe dress fabric
by Zandra Rhodes, 1968. Inspired
by adverts for Christian Dior
beauty products, it was one
of the most popular prints
sold through Rhodes and
Sylvia Ayton's Fulham Road
Clothes Shop.

By 1970 most British artists had disengaged from the design of mass-produced textiles and were concentrating on their core activities of painting and sculpture. A final flickering of the flame came in 1969 when Sonia Delaunay, then aged eighty-four, designed a headsquare for Liberty of London, which, in its elegant abstraction and subtle nuances of colour, is a graceful elegy for textile design as a successful medium for artists in twentieth-century Britain.

37 A silk square, designed by Sonia Delaunay, and produced in a limited edition by Liberty of London, 1969.

The 1960s: America. Serendipity 3, Stephen Bruce and Andy Warhol; Bloomcraft and Picasso; White Stag and Picasso; Piazza Prints and John Rombola

38a and 38b Two dresses designed by Stephen Bruce and his assistant Leila Larmon in the early 1960s using Warhol designs. They were part of a group of food-related fabrics designed by Warhol, and given to Bruce for his newly created Serendipity 3 wholesale fashion business. Courtesy of Stephen Bruce.

1 Stephen Bruce, interview with author, November 2010.

2 Ibid.

3 Ibid.

4 On the cafe's fiftieth anniversary, in 2004, a $1,000 dollar sundae, 'Golden Opulence', was added to the menu, and in 2007 another, 'Frozen Haute Chocolate', at $25,000.

5 Stephen Bruce.

6 Ibid.

7 Ibid.

8 Jesse Kornbluth, *Andy Warhol – Pre-Pop Warhol*, 1988, p. 122. Warhol's commercial studio appears to have functioned until 1965, when Nathan Gluck, his studio assistant, received his last cheque for commercial work.

9 Matt Wrbican, Archivist, the Andy Warhol Museum, Pittsburgh, email correspondence with Richard Chamberlain, 24 January, 2010.

10 Ivan Vartanian, ed., *Andy Warhol, Drawings and Illustrations of the 1950s*, p. 107.

11 Stephen Bruce.

12 Kornbluth, p.126.

13 John Rombola, interview with author, February 2011.

As in Britain, the involvement of artists with commercial textile design drew to a close in America during the 1960s. The decade, however, opened with a remarkable group of fashion fabrics designed by Andy Warhol for his friend Stephen Bruce, proprietor of the legendary New York cafe boutique, Serendipity 3. In the early 1960s Bruce had discussed the possibility of Warhol designing textiles to use for the fashion project he had recently set up. Nothing concrete seemed to come of these occasional discussions until Warhol arrived unexpectedly at Serendipity one day with four or five rolls of textiles.[1]

Founded by Bruce, with two friends, in 1954 on the Upper East Side of Manhattan, Serendipity soon became a fashionable gathering place for New York's bohemian society, and Warhol was a regular visitor throughout his life. In the 1950s he spent many afternoons there, usually bringing his portfolio with him, which often contained rejected drawings for advertisements for companies such as I. Miller Shoes.[2] Bruce suggested selling them in the cafe and recalls how 'Andy', and his 'somewhat exotic entourage', would sit around a table there, randomly adding colour to the drawings with Indian inks – Dr Martin's Aniline Watercolor Dyes – before they were framed and hung for sale. A set-up described by Bruce as very much a precursor of Warhol's 'Silver Factory' in the 1960s.[3]

Serendipity's menu featured iconic American Pop classics such as 'foot long hot dogs', but it was then, and still is, especially noted for its extravagant desserts, particularly elaborate ice cream sundaes.[4] It was against the background of this extremely glamorous Pop milieu – Marilyn Monroe and Jackie Kennedy were among the cafe's customers – that Stephen Bruce took up fashion design, manufacturing the garments on the second floor of the Serendipity building.[5]

Warhol's textile designs for Bruce, two of which were used for a Serendipity fashion collection, were derived from food associated with the cafe. They are in a transitional style prescient of Warhol's later Pop work; one has a pattern of giant pretzels and the other of oversized ice cream cones, and Bruce recalls a third of petit fours. There is another of ice cream sundaes and, although after so long he cannot now be certain, Bruce says there was possibly even a fifth.[6] The designs were drawn using the blotted, broken line typical of Warhol's early graphic work, on plain white backgrounds and vividly coloured with the brilliant Indian inks then favoured by him. The identity of the manufacturer of these remarkable textiles remains unknown. Bruce says Warhol was always extremely secretive in business and never revealed the company's name. Neither did Bruce have any reason to re-order from them as there was little, if any, demand for the dresses which, although 'great fun', few wanted: it seems clothing covered with images of giant pretzels or ice cream cones was not considered quite de rigueur at the time.[7]

The Warhol Museum in Pittsburgh holds samples of other fabrics designed by him, which, although very different to the Pop images of those he gave to Bruce, are prescient of his later depictions of flowers. The museum's samples, like those used by Bruce, date from the commercial phase of his career, up to about 1965,[8] and

'there is no information as to manufacturer or date. Typically, Warhol's business records do not clearly indicate what he was doing for a client … they are extremely vague and very much of the moment.'[9]

In commercial practice Warhol was not in the habit of letting his right hand know what his left hand was doing, keeping art directors and clients away from his studio assistants and vice versa, his assistants rarely knew for what or for whom a piece of work was intended.[10]

Although Bruce never knew who produced the fabrics he had used, he suggests Warhol may have designed more for the same firm. He recalls Warhol as hugely prolific and always ready to take on work, 'Andy had several irons in the fire at all times'.[11] Supporting this view Jesse Kornbluth writes,

'… if Andy Warhol ever turned down any commercial work no one has come forward to reveal that historic moment.'[12]

In a similar vein the New York graphic designer John Rombola, who was personally well acquainted with Warhol in the 1950s, says

'Andy was then completely commercial in outlook and would consider doing any work as long as there was $50 in it for him.'[13]

39 'Water Melons', a printed cotton textile produced by D B Fuller & Co, (Fuller Fabrics) circa 1956.

[14] Ibid.

[15] 'Success is a Job in New York: the Early Art and Business of Andy Warhol', exhibition catalogue, Grey Art Gallery and Study Centre/Carnegie Museum of Art, New York/Pittsburgh, 1989, catalogue entry no. 171.

[16] *Glamour* magazine, December 1960, pp. 112-113.

[17] 'Andy Warhol, His Early Works, 1947 – 1959', exhibition catalogue, compiled by Andreas Brown, Gotham Book Mart Gallery, New York City, 1971, p. 11.

[18] Vartanian, pp. 14-16.

[19] Ibid, pp. 24-25.

[20] Wrbican.

Rombola clearly remembers Warhol designing dress textiles, particularly 'three or four he did for Dan Fuller, somewhere about 1956 or 1957', although he cannot now recall what the designs were, other than a vague memory of their being 'florals'. He was then also aware of other Warhol textile designs depicting butterflies or umbrellas, and of plastic trays decorated with birds in ornamental cages, which were designed by Warhol for the restaurant in the New York department store, Lord & Taylor.[14]

Two cotton fabrics from the 1950s are also known, one with Warhol's 'Happy Bug Day' design and the other with a variation of a companion design, 'Happy Butterfly Day'. Warhol also adapted these designs in the mid-fifties for greetings cards, stationery, and gift-wrap, and there are several references to his creating fabric designs at this time.[15] He continued to recycle the butterfly motif, a particular favourite of his, for a variety of purposes throughout the later 1950s, using a version of it in 1960 for the design of a particularly outstanding fashion textile, 'Bright Butterflies'.[16] The textile, manufactured by Nat Wager, was used for dresses and blouses designed by Robert Sloan which were featured in the December 1960 issue of *Glamour* magazine. There is also a dynamic border print, in the same distinctive colourway as the 'Happy Bug Day' textile, with the design of a clown riding on the shoulders of an, apparently, old Russian babushka, who in turn stands on the back of a galloping horse, while above the clown leaps and turns somersaults in a series of simple kinetic freeze-frames. This image of the clown is a variation of that originally devised by Warhol, in about 1950-51, for a proposed, but unpublished, Christmas card for Robert Macgregor of New Directions Publishing, New York.[17] The textile's design is close in style to Warhol's illustrations for children's books in the 1950s,[18] the horse being particularly reminiscent of many similar images by him.[19] Throughout his commercial career Warhol recycled and redrew images to create pattern designs for a wide variety of purposes, including textiles.

"Some of Warhol's pattern designs may have been created for gift-wrap, rather than fabric. They may also have been used for both these end products. The artist was always happy to oblige a paying client."[20]

40 A group of five fashion textiles designed by Andy Warhol from the collection of the Warhol Museum, Pittsburgh. These stylised floral patterns, dating from circa 1957, were possibly produced by Fuller Fabrics. Courtesy of the Warhol Museum, Pittsburgh.

41 Next spread Fashion textile depicting various ice cream sundaes, early 1960s.

42 Previous page left A printed cotton fashion textile, circa 1955. This is one of Warhol's most famous designs, 'Happy Bug Day', which was originally conceived as a greetings card in 1954. Similarly, versions of his 'Happy Butterfly Day' design of the same year were printed onto cotton for apparel yardage, stationery and three-dimensional screens.

43 Previous page right Textile with a variation of Warhol's 'Happy Butterfly Day' design, second half of the 1950s.

44 Previous page right, inset Illustration from a fashion article in *Glamour*, December 1960, entitled 'Sunning; Bright Butterflies', with textiles designed by Andy Warhol and printed by Nat Wager. The garments were designed by Robert Sloan and sold through, amongst others, Saks, New York.

45 A cotton border print, circa 1955. The origins of this textile can be traced back to sketches executed by Warhol in 1951 for proposed designs for a group of Christmas cards for Robert McGregor, of New Directions Publishing.

46 Serendipity 3, the facade of Steven Bruce's New York café. Bruce can be seen through the open door and Andy Warhol is pictured sitting outside. Courtesy of Stephen Bruce.

In 1963, 'Bloomcraft Fabrics' launched a group of eleven furnishing textiles, 'The Picasso Collection' – the result of a collaboration between Picasso and Bloomcraft's design studio.

Similar in many ways to the project that Picasso had been involved with at Fuller Fabrics in 1954, but on a more spectacular scale: the Bloomcraft designs were taken from a wide spectrum of Picasso's oeuvre and silk-screen printed on a variety of materials in sumptuous colourways. Bloomcraft, a New York-based company founded by Sidney Bloom, had some experience of working with artists: in 1950 it had commissioned textile designs from the painter and printmaker Rockwell Kent, for 'The Happily Married Collection', including 'Deer Season' and 'Harvest Time',[21] but the sheer scope and scale of the Picasso project far exceeded that in its verve and brio.

The collection received considerable publicity at its launch, with a well-orchestrated advertising campaign and feature articles in leading magazines; *American Fabrics*, announced that 'a carefully selected number of leading stores from coast to coast will launch this unique home furnishings collection during early fall' and that the fabrics 'will retail at approximately $5 dollars a yard'.[22]

PICASSO OLÉ!

If the ordinary bores you and the imaginative stirs your soul, this decorative fabric collection was designed for you...as vital, daring and provocative as the Master himself. And the cloth is protected by DuPont's Ze pel® fluoridizer that makes it stain resistant and water repellent. At the fine stores listed on the facing page. BLOOMCRAFT FABRICS

Picasso's wry sense of humour was particularly in evidence in a feature in *Look*, where it was announced the textiles were suitable for:

"every form of interior decoration, except upholstery. By the maestro's wishes, Picasso's may be leaned against, not sat on."[23]

A further, rather improbable, textile project also took place in 1963 between Picasso and the Oregon-based sportswear manufacturer, White Stag. The project was the brainchild of two optimistic San Francisco-based 'Ad men', Howard Grossage and Bob Freeman, who, undeterred by an earlier disastrous attempt at marketing culture to the masses by selling sweatshirts adorned with images of composers such as Bach, Brahms and Beethoven, decided 'Fine Art' was the thing and, having first come to an understanding with White Stag, went to France to meet Picasso. They never did, but eventually made a deal with him, through his Parisian representatives, for White Stag to have exclusive rights to use certain of his designs on fabric.[24]

By the 1960s, White Stag was the leading manufacturer of mass-produced clothing for

47 Right Advertisement for Bloomcraft Fabrics, circa 1963, featuring three of the eleven designs by Picasso: 'Posters of Picasso', 'Toros y Toreros' and 'Musical Fawn'.

48 Opposite 'Posters of Picasso', printed cotton furnishing fabric, produced by Bloomcraft, circa 1963.

[21] Collection, the Art Institute of Chicago, accession nos. 1977.182 and 1977.183.

[22] *American Fabrics*, no. 61, summer 1963, p. 76.

[23] *Look*, December 1963, M5.

[24] Eugenia Sheppard, 'Inside Fashion', the *New York Herald Tribune*, June 1963.

recreational skiing in the United States. An interest in skiing had grown rapidly in Oregon in the 1930s and White Stag's ski wear quickly gained a reputation, especially in the western states. After the Second World War the sport skyrocketed in popularity and with it sales of White Stag's ski clothing. The contract with Picasso was a major coup for the company, who produced a range of fashionable après-ski wear in collaboration with the artist.

The range consisted of PVC coated rainwear, ski jackets and anoraks, printed corduroy ponchos, shirts, blouses and sweatshirts, even a hostess 'culottes' dress, all priced between $9 and $30.[25] Although White Stag subsequently publicised the range widely, until the moment of the launch, it was kept under tight wraps, referred to only by the code name, Project Marvin. The range was eventually announced in the *New York Herald Tribune* in June 1963 in 'Inside Fashion', the column of the well-known fashion writer, Eugenia Sheppard, who gave a detailed account of the range's genesis and Picasso's involvement. The company also conducted an extensive advertising campaign, with each item in the range described in detail and, to further facilitate sales, a booklet on Picasso and his work was provided for the education of the sales people involved. There is little or no information concerning the project's success, but, judging from the scarcity of surviving pieces, it does not appear to have been a triumph. It seems such projects were more often a puff for a company than a serious commercial venture, essentially a form of 'loss-leader'.

Picasso was apparently very taken with the idea of his work being used for sportswear, probably the principal motivation behind his involvement with White Stag, (for he was certainly neither in need of money nor publicity). His involvement paralleled the earlier radical ideas on fashion of avant-garde artists and designers such as the Russian Constructivist El Lissitsky or the Italian Futurist Giacomo Balla. Particularly relevant in this context are the extraordinary designs of the Constructivist Vavara Stepanova for inexpensive mass produced sportswear that was widely disseminated in Paris during the 1925 Exposition Internationale des Arts Décoratifs et Industriels Modernes. Something which Picasso – the twentieth century's leading avant-garde artist, lifelong sympathizer with socialist ideals, and a fully paid up member of the French Communist Party – would have been well aware.

Following the Second World War, a sharp edged, sophisticated and witty style of graphic design and illustration evolved in New York,

which, although considerably indebted to the work of Saul Steinberg, also owed much to that of the artists Ben Shahn and Paul Klee. It was widely influential and many artists and designers in the 1950s and 1960s, from Andy Warhol to Ronald Searle and Roland Emmet in Britain, developed their own personal versions. One outstanding exponent is the New York artist, graphic designer and illustrator John Rombola who, like Steinberg and Warhol, is very much a Renaissance man. His work encompasses many aspects of design, from small printed vignettes to stage sets and costumes, and even fashion.[26]

In 1956 Rombola's agent suggested he attend an interview with Mr Piazza and Mr Smith of Harben Papers, who were looking for someone of originality and exceptional graphic talent to work on their ranges of furnishing fabrics and wallpapers. Harben Papers turned out to be a satellite of Patterson Fabrics, a subsidiary of Piazza Prints, set up by Mr Piazza in the previous decade to manufacture exclusive wallpapers and fabrics for upmarket interior decorators.[27] In the later 1940s and early 1950s, Piazza Prints and Patterson Fabrics had developed a range of wallpapers and textiles designed by Saul Steinberg, in which they made a considerable long-term financial investment.

By 1956 the company's relationship with Steinberg had broken down and they were seeking a suitable replacement.[28] Following a successful interview with Rombola, they immediately engaged him on a freelance basis. Between 1956 and 1968 he created twelve successful designs for the company that were produced both as textiles and wallpapers.[29] The designs, remarkable examples of Rombola's highly original style, draw on a wide range of subject matter, from 'Circus', 1956, and 'Cat and Canary', 1958, to 'Alice in Wonderland' and 'Egypt', both 1968.

Other textile companies Rombola worked for were the upmarket New York manufacturer, Arundell Clarke, and, at around the same time in 1956, he also made several designs for Fuller Fabrics, whose Modern Masters range of dress fabrics designed by, amongst others, Picasso and Miro, he greatly admired. His last textile designs were for domestic linens manufactured by Martex for Marcus Niemann in the late 1970s.

Few, if any, industrially manufactured textiles designed by artists were produced in America after the 1960s. One notable exception was Circus Acrobats designed by Alexander Calder shortly before his death, to coincide with his retrospective exhibition, 'Calder's Universe', held at the Whitney Museum of American Art, New York, in 1976.

49 A Picasso design on plastic coated cotton, used for an après-ski jacket, produced by White Stag, 1963.

25 Ibid.

26 For the launch of the book *John Rombola, Eclectic Eccentric*, in 2010, he was commissioned to design five window displays for the New York Fifth Avenue department store, Bergdorf Goodman.

27 Rombola.

28 Ibid.

29 Ibid.

50a and 50b 'Frontispiece', was designed by Picasso for Bloomcraft Fabrics, as a furnishing fabric, circa 1963, but was also used by Alice Polynesian Fashions, for summer clothing such as this shift dress. 'Musical Fawn', was also used for fashion garments.

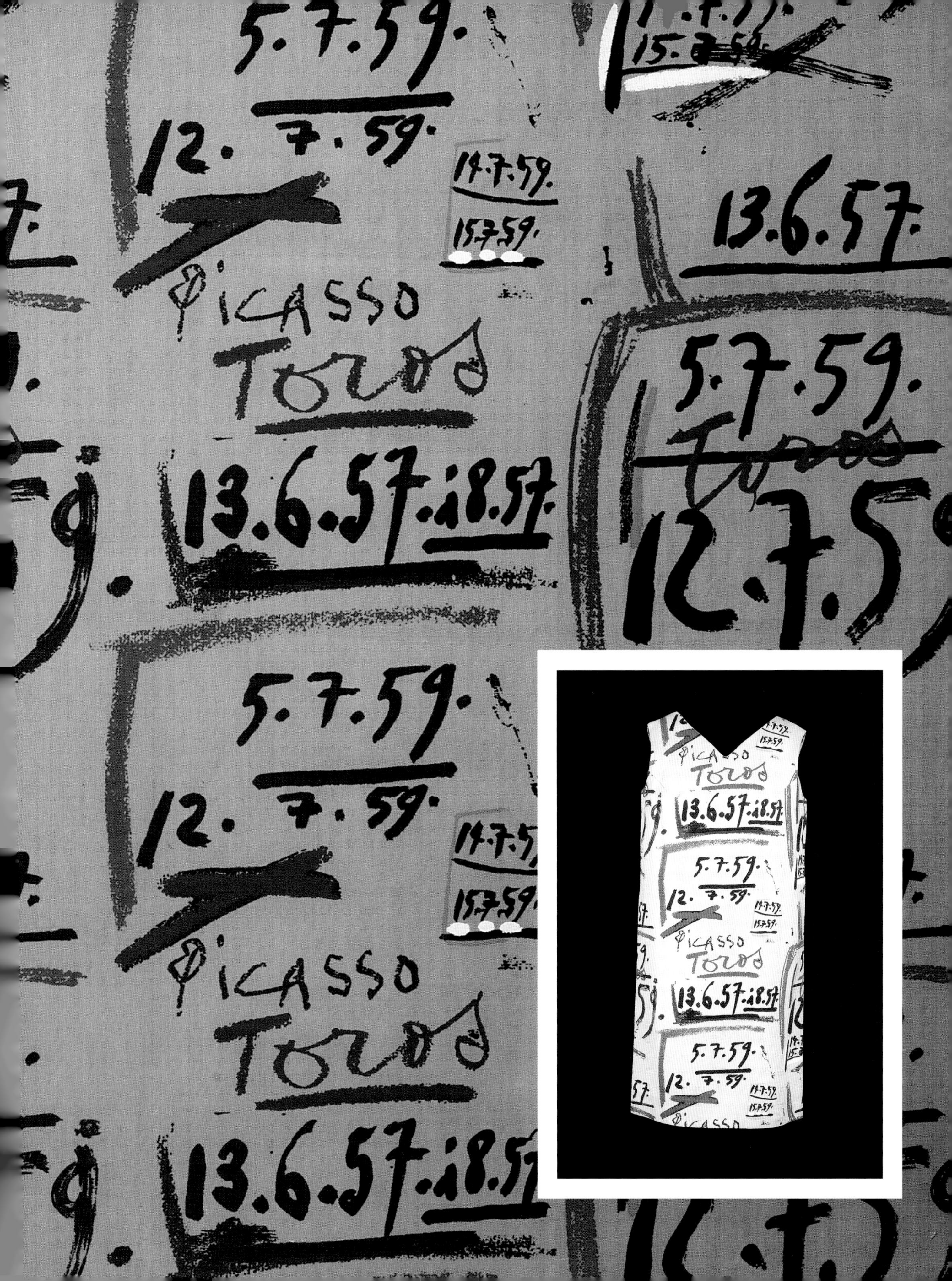
5.7.59.
12.7.59.
14.7.59.
15.7.59.
PICASSO
Toros
13.6.57.18.57.
13.6.57.

51 'Still Life', by Picasso for
Bloomcraft Fabrics, circa 1963.

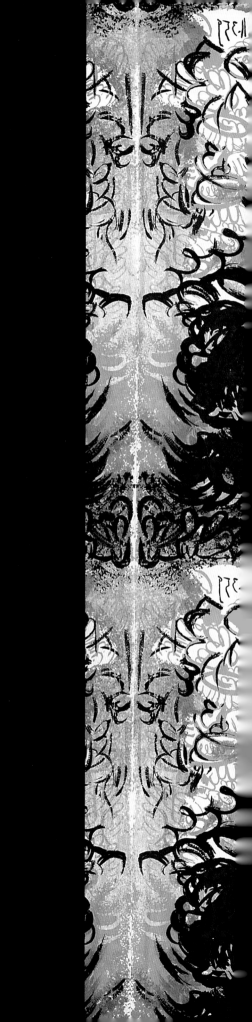

52 'Carnet II', by Picasso for
Bloomcraft Fabrics, circa 1963.

53 'Musical Fawn', by Picasso for
Bloomcraft Fabrics, circa 1963.

56 'Sketchbook', by Picasso
for Bloomcraft Fabrics,

circa 1963.

57 'Figures', shirting fabric produced by White Stag from a design by Picasso, 1963, was one of a small group that also included a dramatic dress using a Picasso 'Clown' design and produced under White Stag's West House Juniors label.

58 'Circus', the first textile design by John Rombola to be produced by Patterson Fabrics, 1956. Rombola's designs were also produced as wallpapers by Patterson's sister companies, Piazza Prints and Harben Papers.

59 'Parade', by Rombola for Patterson Fabrics, 1957, was also printed as a wallpaper by Piazza Prints.

60 Showing the clear
influence of Psychedelia,
John Rombola's 'Alice In
Wonderland' was produced
by Patterson/Piazza, 1968.
Courtesy of the Cooper
Hewitt Museum, New York.

61 'Cat & Canary' designed by John Rombola for Patterson/Harben Papers, 1959. Courtesy of the Cooper Hewitt Museum, New York.

62 Following Page Screen-printed textile, depicting circus acrobats, designed by Alexander Calder and produced for the Whitney Museum, 1976. The museum held a major retrospective; 'Calder's Universe' in this year and Calder worked with the Whitney on preparations, including this textile design, before his untimely death five weeks after the exhibition opened.

Like Sonia Delaunay's headsquare for Liberty of London in 1969, Calder's final textile provides an appropriate swansong for the distinguished series of textiles designed by artists in America for the mass market between the 1920s and 1960s, which were truly an art for the people.

APPENDICES

BIOGRAPHIES

Ascher (London) Ltd

Founded in 1942 by Zika (1910-92) and Lida (d.1983) Ascher, who had moved to London following the annexation of their home country, Czechoslovakia, in 1933. The firm originally bought in fabrics which were printed in their workshops, but soon began weaving and printing their own fabrics for the couture trade. By the time of their closure they had produced almost every fabric type imaginable. The company was central to the development of dress- and coat-weight chenilles; innovatory printing techniques for nylon; new silk weaves and the development of non-woven fabrics and printed paper dresses. Their first range of Modernist fabrics was launched in 1942. Ascher commissioned designs from many important artists from 1943 but launched their first printed silk artist headsquares at 'Britain Can Make It', 1946. All the leading couture houses including Chanel, Molyneux, Schiaparelli, Cardin, Balmain, Griffe, Dior, Balenciaga, Givenchy and many others used Ascher fabrics. The artists they commissioned included Sutherland, Calder, Picabia, Sigmund Politzer, Barry Kay, Hepworth, Ben Nicholson, Piper, Cocteau, Hitchens, Colquhoun, Scottie Wilson, Vaughan, de Staël, Jean Hugo, Derain, Trevelyan and the Polish émigré, Topolski. Moore and Matisse also produced designs for huge printed linen wall hangings for Ascher in 1948, which were exhibited at the Lefevre Gallery, London, in 1947.

Associated American Artists

The gallery was founded as a commercial art venture by Reeves Lewenthal in 1934. Lewenthal's journalism and public relations background helped him see the potential in promoting reasonably priced signed artists' prints, at the same time helping the artists realise some income. His first prints, commissioned in 1934, were sold through retail stores and by mail order and by the end of the thirties he had opened a gallery in New York's Fifth Avenue. After the Second World War Associated American Artists' (AAA) new galleries stocked increasingly 'Modern' and often abstract art, and tried to engage with new ideas and explore new ways to promote (or exploit) art and artists. During the 1950s Lewenthal's gallery became increasingly involved with new areas for artists to work in, particularly in the design of ceramics, under the label Stonelain, textiles and other homeware. They commissioned designs for textiles from many successful American and European artists and designers including Vincent Malta,

Arnold Blanch, Doris Lee, John Hull, Hans Moller, Laura Jean Allen and Jacqueline Groag. These artists' designs were marketed as 'Signature Fine Art Fabrics', and were manufactured by M Lowenstein & Sons (dress fabrics) and Riverdale Manufacturing Co. (furnishing fabrics) from circa 1952-57. AAA was hugely successful and was much copied by other companies. In 1958 Lewenthal split away from AAA to go to Rust Craft Greeting Cards, taking with him the decorative arts production, and leaving Sylvan Cole to continue the fine art gallery business.

Christian Bérard
1902-1949

A painter, graphic designer and theatre designer, Bérard's first exhibition was at the Galerie Druet in 1924. He was a regular contributor to *Vogue*. Designed the sets and costumes for the Ballets Russes which toured the USA and South America and for Jean Cocteau's *La Machine infernale* and acted as artistic director for Cocteau's 1946 film *La Belle et la Bête*. Bérard produced designs for tapestries for Jean-Michel Frank in the 1930s, as well as carpets made by Maurice Lauer at Aubusson & Cogolin. Martin Battersby called Bérard the 'most influential designer of the thirties' whose advice and approval were sought by dressmakers, interior designers and leaders of fashion. In the 1940s he designed fashion fabrics and silk squares for Ascher Ltd.

Bianchini-Férier

The company was established in Lyons, France, in 1888 as Atuyer, Bianchini, Férier by three men who had worked in the city's renowned silk industry. They set out to produce high fashion dress silks and quickly expanded their manufacturing and commercial premises. In Paris their sales office was located strategically close to the couture quarter and by 1920, as well as sales representatives throughout Europe, Bianchini-Férier, had permanent offices in Brussels, New York and London. They later expanded into other parts of America including South America and began manufacturing in New York in 1921. From the 1920s the firm also produced block-printed linen and cotton furnishing fabrics at their factory in Tournon. In 1912 the firm signed an exclusive contract with Raoul Dufy who had been producing fabrics for Paul Poiret's atelier. The company's relationship with Dufy lasted sixteen years and produced in excess of 4000 designs. Other artists who designed for Bianchini included Alberto Lorenzi, Jean Beaumont, the illustrator Robert Bonfils,

Paul Mansouroff and artist-designer, Peter Todd Mitchell, who produced scarf designs during the 1950s. The firm still has its headquarters in Lyon and is thought to be the longest continuously-running mill in Europe.

Bloomcraft Fabrics Inc.

A New York based textile converter founded and run by Sidney Bloom. Their 1950 'Happily Married' range contained a number of furnishing fabrics designed by the painter and printmaker Rockwell Kent including 'Deer Season' and 'Harvest Time'. In the early 1960s they worked with Picasso to create a series of screen-printed furnishing textiles in a variety of fabrics and finishes. Gloria Vanderbilt, the heiress and socialite, designed for Bloomcraft in the late 1960s after studying at the Art Students League of New York. The company, now referred to as Bloomcraft Home Fashions, is a division of P Kaufman Inc. and focuses mainly on woven textiles.

Martin Bradley
b.1931

A painter, potter and printmaker, born in Richmond, Middlesex, England, Bradley ran away and joined the Merchant Navy and later the Spanish Foreign Legion. He travelled extensively in India and the Far East. A self-taught artist, he was in contact with the Soho artists in the 1950s and had his first solo exhibition at Gimpel Fils in 1954. A number of his lithographs were published by the Curwen Press and during the 1950s he also designed and produced studio ceramics. Bradley was influenced by American comic strips, oriental calligraphy, graffiti and figurative images. He designed furnishing textiles for Liberty & Co. from 1955-57.

Georges Braque
1882-1963

A major twentieth-century French painter and sculptor who, with Picasso, developed Cubism, Braque came from a family of house decorators, and initially trained as such, but he also studied painting at the École des Beaux-Arts and was influenced by the Fauves. During the 1940s and 1950s he created many lithographs and book illustrations. He and Picasso were very close and it was probably through Picasso that Fuller contacted Braque and produced textiles to his design for the 'Modern Masters Range' in 1956. Braque's decorative *oeuvre* was far reaching including tapestries, ceramics, designs for two Diaghilev ballets, stained glass for the church at Varengeville, a decorated ceiling for the Louvre, Paris, and in the last year of his life he created a number of jewellery designs with Baron Herger de Lowenfeld.

Alexander Calder
1898-1976

Born into a family of sculptors and artists, Calder was the American sculptor and artist who invented the mobile. He studied mechanical engineering at the Stevens Institute of Technology and worked for some time as an engineer before enrolling at the Art Students League of New York with the intention of following an artistic career. Whilst in Paris in the 1920s he met Joan Miró, Jean Arp and Marcel Duchamp and was inspired by Piet Mondrian's abstract work; he began to experiment with making toys and kinetic sculpture. As well as his sculptures, both static and mobile, he also created paintings, lithographs, tapestries and jewellery some of which was included in the Goldsmiths' Hall 'International Jewellery Exhibition 1890-1961' at their London headquarters in 1961. Calder's 'La Mer' silk square, for Ascher was produced in 1947 but he also created two designs for textiles and wallpapers for Laverne Originals in 1949: 'Splotchy' and 'Calder No.1'. In later life Calder designed rugs that were hand-hooked by his wife, Louisa, as well as a screen-printed silk scarf design for Galerie Adrien Maeght, Paris, produced by Maison Brochier in 1969, and woven sisal hangings circa 1967. In 1976, shortly before his death, the Whitney Museum of American Art issued a printed cotton fabric 'Acrobats' to celebrate his retrospective 'Calder's Universe'.

George Campbell
1917-1979

An artist and designer born into a family of artists in Arklow, Ireland, Campbell was educated in Belfast, Dublin and at La Grande Chaumière, Paris. Campbell's influences were the Spanish and Irish landscapes. He was acknowledged as an important ecumenical artist, winning the Sacred Art Award in 1962, although he was also known for on-the-set drawings for film premieres. He designed stained glass for Galway Cathedral and four of his paintings, exhibited in 'Living Art' 1969, were made into textiles by David Whitehead Ltd.

Jon Catleugh
1920-2009

Born in King's Lynn, Norfolk, Catleugh was an architect, painter, designer, collagist, theatre designer and ceramic historian. He was influenced by an exhibition of Jackson Pollock's work in Venice in 1949 and exhibited at 'British Abstract Art' in 1951. Described as part of the 1950s 'Tachiste Tornado' by Herbert Read, he held his first one-man exhibition at Gimpel Fils,

1953. He exhibited at a number of influential exhibitions including 'Painting into Textiles', 1953, 'This is Tomorrow' and 'Tomorrow's Furniture'. He worked in the Schools Department of the London County Council Architects' Department; as Furniture Adviser to the War Office and as Design Director at Conran from 1961-2. Catleugh designed the set for Picasso's play *Desire Caught by the Tail* at the Watergate Theatre, 1951. He designed fabrics for David Whitehead Ltd, who had purchased three of his paintings and collages from 'Painting into Textiles', and had a 'Tachiste' painting adapted for a fashion silk by Sekers. Always an inveterate collector, in later life he became an expert on William De Morgan ceramics and a trustee of the William De Morgan Foundation.

Marc Chagall
1887-1985
A pioneer of Modernism and one of the most successful twentieth-century artists, Chagall worked in almost every medium. He was born into a poor Hasidic Jewish family in Russia and was initially self-taught. He moved to St Petersburg in 1906 and studied under Leon Bakst. By 1910 he was ready to move on to Paris where he became associated with Guillaume Apollinaire, Fernand Léger and Robert Delaunay. Chagall split his time between France and Russia, until in 1941 he was forced to leave Europe to escape the Nazi extermination of Jews and their dislike of progressive artists. In 1941 with the help of Alfred Barr from the Museum of Modern Art Chagall moved to New York. After the war Chagall returned to France. Outside of his work in fine art Chagall designed stained glass; sets and costumes for ballet and stage; ceramics; large ceramic murals as well as making and painting pots. He designed tapestries woven under the direction of Yvette Cauquil-Prince, who had also collaborated with Picasso. Only 40 of his tapestries were ever to reach the commercial market. He designed three tapestries as well as twelve floor mosaics and a wall mosaic for the State Hall of the Knesset, Israel. Fuller Fabrics produced Chagall's designs as dress and furnishing fabrics as part of their Modern Masters Range in 1950s.

Geoffrey Clarke
b.1924
Sculptor, painter, enamellist, printmaker and designer, Clarke was born in Darley Dale, Derbyshire, and educated at Preston and Manchester Schools of Art. After war service Clarke studied at Lancaster and Morecambe School of Art and at the Royal College of Art, London, where he started in the stained glass department. He became interested in sculpture but since this department was principally interested in clay and plaster he made his forged and welded iron sculptures in the wood, metals and plastics department. Clarke's first exhibition was at Gimpel Fils in 1952. He developed an interest in prints mainly to use as studies for his sculptures. Clarke made all types and sizes of three-dimensional metal objects including pulpits and altar rails, silver beer mugs, silver altar crosses, candlesticks and fonts. He supplied large open cast reliefs to the cruise ships *Canberra* and *Oriana*, and stained glass to Coventry Cathedral and Newnham College, Cambridge amongst others. One of his prints was transferred on to plastic laminate and incorporated into a cabinet designed by Robin Day. The cabinet, included in a room set by Day, was awarded a gold medal at the Milan Triennale in 1951. Clarke's work was exhibited at the Festival of Britain, 1951, and he was the most prolific contributor of art works to the newly restored Coventry Cathedral, consecrated in 1962. Clarke had two of his prints worked into textiles by Edinburgh Weavers: 'Grape' and 'The Dolmen', both circa 1957; he also designed two wallpapers for Sanderson & Co, an anaglypta and a flock paper.

Jean Cocteau
1889-1963
Painter, designer, poet, playwright, film-maker, novelist and sculptor, born in Maisons-Laffitte, France, Cocteau was renowned for his intellectual pursuits and was acquainted with many of the leading artists including Picasso and Modigliani. His work was associated with the Cubist and Surrealist movements although it did not really follow either. In the 1930s Cocteau collaborated with Elsa Schiaparelli on couture collections, and designed 'Masks', a printed silk crepe which was used for an evening dress by the Anglo-American couturier Charles James in 1939. During the 1940s he created designs for jewellery in gold and silver for his friend François Hugo and designed headsquares for Ascher Ltd. Between 1957 and 1963 he made pottery and during the 1950s designed ceramics for Rosenthal AG, Germany, and silverware for Christofle. Cocteau designed numerous theatrical and ballet sets and worked with Diaghilev, Stravinsky and Satie. Simultaneously he created appliqué embroideries and ceramic designs for Atelier Madeleine Jolly and is known to have designed at least one rug for Galerie Cuttoli-Weil.

Cohama Upholstery & Drapery Fabrics
Founded in 1912, Cohama was the brand name for Cohn-Hall-Marx, New York, a division of United Merchants & Manufacturing Inc. In the second half of the 1940s Cohama produced textiles designed by Angelo Testa, some of which he had produced during his time studying at the Chicago Bauhaus, 1942-1943. The company subsequently branched out into dress fabrics, making ties and scarves. Their furnishing fabrics were later marketed as Cohama Riverdale.

Harold Cohen
b.1928
A painter and designer born London, Harold is the brother of painter Bernard Cohen. After studying at the Slade School of Art, 1948-52, he spent time in Italy. From 1954 he held a series of solo exhibitions at Gimpel Fils and the Robert Fraser Gallery. Cohen was a leading member of the 'Situation' group of painters who created very large abstract paintings and in the 1960s represented Great Britain at a number of international shows including the Venice Biennale. He spent time and also exhibited in the USA. In the late 1950s he designed at least two textiles for Heal's as well as several pieces of furniture. The Edinburgh Tapestry Company produced five tapestries to Cohen's designs in the 1960s, one of which was commissioned for British Petroleum's new headquarters, Britannic House, and one for the Victoria and Albert Museum, London. From the 1970s he became very interested in computers and art and has written extensively on artificial intelligence and drawing.

Trevor Coleman
b.1936
Artist, photographer, potter, teacher, editor, Coleman was born in Johannesburg, South Africa to a film-maker father and artist mother. He studied art at Johannesburg Technicon. He began painting professionally in 1959 and subsequently in 1961-2 he attended the Central School of Arts and Crafts in London. Interested in, and influenced by, archaeology, geology, anthropology and African art, having travelled extensively in Africa, his pictures are colourful and hard-edged. Coleman taught in Johannesburg, ran his own gallery for a time and edited *Gallery* magazine. He exhibited widely in Africa and in Britain. Coleman designed screen-printed textiles for Hull Traders Ltd in the 1960s.

Cecil Collins
1908-1989
Collins was an English artist associated for some time with the Surrealist Movement. He was born in Plymouth and began his working life as a mechanic in Devonport. In 1927 he won a scholarship to the RCA where he was awarded the William Rothenstein Life Drawing Prize. He and his wife lived near Dartington Hall during the later 1930s and were close to the influential American abstract expressionist painter, Mark Tobey, and, undoubtedly, the other outstanding thinkers and artists of their time that gathered there. In 1947 Collins published *Vision of the Fool* a collection of related drawings and paintings that he used to explore spiritualism in the modern age. Collins taught at the Central School of Art from 1951-75 where he influenced emerging young artists. His decorative work included a number of commissions for the Church of England and for the Edinburgh Tapestry Company during the 1950s, as well as book illustration. He designed textiles for Edinburgh Weavers including 'Avon', 1959, initially commissioned for use in the conference hall of the British Embassy in Washington, USA.

Cresta Silks Ltd.
Cresta was founded in Welwyn Garden City, England, in 1929 by Tom Heron (1890-1983) who was descended from a family of weavers. Heron had worked as managing director for Alec Walker at Crystéde Textiles, Newlyn 1926-29. After a disagreement with Walker, Heron set up Cresta Silks. His interests in art, particularly with the Leeds Art Club, and politics brought him into contact with a number of avant-garde artists, including the Nashs, Spencers, Nevinson, Gilman, Gore and Ginner. After the Second World War Patrick Heron, Tom's son, became the principal designer for the firm which by this time was producing both fashion and furnishing fabrics. Amongst other artists who also designed for the company were Graham Sutherland, Mary Duncan and Lana Mackinnon. When Crystéde was liquidated, Cresta bought many of their blocks which they put into use. As a conscientious objector during the World Wars, Tom Heron was invited to join the 'Board of Trade' as Adviser on Women's and Children's Clothing, and he developed the Utility Clothing Scheme, involving the leading designers Digby Morton, Hardy Amies and Edward Molyneux, which became the model for other utility schemes. Tom Heron slowly withdrew his involvement from the firm during the 1950s and the company was sold.

Cr: séde Textiles

Alec Walker established Cryséde in Newlyn, Cornwall in 1923 to produce block-printed artist-designed dress fabrics. Walker came from an old established family of Yorkshire silk weavers but had moved down to Cornwall to pursue an artistic career, and became friends with Frank Dobson, Ernest and Dod Proctor and Cedric Morris. Walker began designing fauvist-inspired textiles himself after discussions with Raoul Dufy in Paris. In 1926 the company relocated to larger premises in St Ives and Walker was joined by Tom Heron who co-managed the company which had expanded to include a chain of retail outlets by the early 1930s. In 1933 Walker and Heron parted company, the latter to set up the rival company of Cresta Silks, and in 1941 Cryséde went into voluntary liquidation.

Mitzi Cunliffe
1918-2006

A sculptor, designer and teacher born in New York, Cunliffe studied at Columbia University, USA, and in Sweden and France. She lived in Manchester, Brighton and London from 1949-74. Her impression of Chartres Cathedral inspired her to dedicate her career to creating sculpture for architecture. Her work includes many free-standing sculptures as well as mural reliefs. Cunliffe was commissioned to design the extraordinary bronze door handles in the shape of hands for the House & Garden Pavilion at the Festival of Britain, 1951, by Misha Black. She designed a number of textiles for Tootal Broadhurst, a special textile for Queen Elizabeth's Coronation, 1953, and furnishing fabrics for David Whitehead Ltd. In 1955 she designed the mask trophy for the BAFTA Awards; modern free-form bowls for Pilkington's Royal Lancastrian Ceramics, and jewellery for friends and clients some of which was exhibited at Goldsmiths' Hall's pioneering 'International Exhibition of Modern Jewellery 1890-1961'. During the 1970s she taught architectural ceramics and sculptural design at Thames Polytechnic.

Salvador Dalí
1904-1989

A painter, film-maker and sculptor who designed sets for stage, film and opera, Dalí was born in Catalonia, Spain, close to the French border. He was an eccentric art student in Madrid in the 1920s and established himself as an accomplished painter and draughtsman in the Surrealist manner, often collaborating with other artists. Dalí worked in many mediums throughout his life and his work includes designs for silver and jewellery, his famous lobster telephone and the Mae West lips sofa for Edward James; he also collaborated in a number of films. He was a prolific textile designer during the 1940s working for Wesley Simpson, Schiffer Prints and producing scarf designs for the World of Silk and the International Silk Congress, in 1950 and 1957, both of which were featured on the cover of *American Fabrics*. His carpet designs were produced by Mohawk; in 1955 he designed a scarf featuring rhino horns, 'Blue Horns'; and the following year other textiles featuring rhino horns, and horses, for Martha Mills Textile Co. and textiles for Sterling. Other design work included a wrapper for Chupa Chups Lollypops and bottles for Rosso Antico. Ties to his designs were produced by a number of companies including J C Penneys, McCurach and Haband.

Gordon Dent
b.1923

After leaving the army in 1947 Gordon Dent obtained a grant that allowed him to attend Hammersmith School of Art where he achieved a National Diploma in design and went on to teacher training college. He exhibited paintings in London art galleries throughout the 1950s and 1960s including Heals, the Drian Gallery, Walker's Gallery, the Redfern Gallery and a one man show at the Comedy Gallery, Haymarket in 1960. His work was included in the 'New Vision' touring exhibition in 1960, several 'Free Painters Group' exhibitions and was exhibited in Germany and Australia. Dent produced three designs for Heals: 'Voyagers', 1958, picked out by the Council of Industrial Design's newsletter as 'particularly noteworthy', was printed in several colourways on both cotton and satinised cotton; 'Pavonian Spray', 1959, was printed in four colourways at 24/9 per yard; and 'Thistle', 1961, which was an adaptation of his painting 'Crinoid.' In 1962 Arthur H Lee & Son, Birkenhead, translated one of Dent's paintings into a tapestry. He taught pottery and painting from 1953 until his retirement.

André Derain
1880-1954

Sculptor, painter, designer and printmaker, born in Chatou, France, Derain was taught painting by Jacomine, a friend of Cézanne, and studied at the École des Mines, Paris and the Académie Carrière. During 1903-4 he became influenced by Negro Art, and by the work of his close friends, Vlaminck, Matisse, Picasso and Braque. He produced a few pieces of sculpture early on in his career, then little until after 1939 when he began producing terracotta figures and reliefs inspired by ancient sculpture. In 1906 he visited London and produced his Thames series. He painted a large mural for the barracks at Commercy and worked as an illustrator, often under the pseudonym Bouzi. In 1918 he made a series of masks from shells and designed costumes and sets for the Durec Troupe and Diaghilev's Ballets Russes. His rug designs of the late 1920s and early 1930s were made by Maison Mybor and later, after the war, by Galerie Cuttoli-Weil. During the 1940s Derain designed jewellery in bronze, gold and silver that was made by François Hugo. He designed silk squares for Ascher in 1947.

Raoul Dufy
1877-1953

French Fauvist painter who after first designing textiles for the couturier Paul Poiret, was contracted from 1912 to 1928 to design textiles exclusively for the lyon based silk manufacturer Bianchini-Férier . He produced more than 4000 textile designs for Férier that were to prove hugely influential in the field of pattern design. Dufy was later involved in a less successful textile project with Onondaga Silk Co, 1930-33, and although this project was abandoned he continued to work in the decorative arts, including in ceramics during the twenties and thirties – as well as painting – until his death. In 1955 his drawings and gouaches were posthumously reinterpreted by Fuller Fabrics, USA, as part of their signature range of 'Modern Master Prints' under the direction of his widow.

Edinburgh Weavers Ltd

Initially founded 1928 by James Morton (1867-1943) in Edinburgh as part of Morton Sundour Fabrics (founded 1914), the company moved to Carlisle, Cumbria, England, in 1930. James's son, Alastair Morton (1910-1963), himself a painter, was responsible for commissioning and producing designs in the 1930s when the firm established itself as a leading manufacturer of avant-garde, Modernist rugs and fabrics. The Edinburgh Weavers 'Constructivist' range, launched in October 1937, included designs by Barbara Hepworth, Winifred Nicholson, Ashley Havinden, Eileen Holding, Arthur Jackson, Jake Nicholson and no less than three by Ben Nicholson. Alastair Morton also supplied designs to Horrockses Fashions Ltd for their ready-to-wear collections during the 1940s. His close friendship with Ben Nicholson, his interest in artists' designs and knowledge of weaving, learnt from Ethel Mairet, ensured a continued interest post-war when the firm bought a number of paintings from the 'Painting into Textiles' exhibition, 1953. These were translated into fabrics, and recommended the commissioning of designs from artists. Edinburgh Weavers produced an enormous range of artist-designed fabrics by Geoffrey Clarke, Keith Vaughan, Marino Marini, Alan Reynolds, William Scott, Elizabeth Frink, Dennis Hawkins, Dusan Dzamonja, Cesar, Charles Raymond, Victor Vasarely, Friedlinde de Colbertado Dinzl, Robert McGowan, Hans Tisdall, Anthony Harrison, Edward Middleditch, Kenneth Rowntree, Joe Tilson, Scottie Wilson, Cliff Holden, Humphrey Spender, Robert Tierney, William Gear, Trevor Bates and Cecil Collins. They received much praise for their inventive designs and avant-garde fabrics from the 1930s through to the 1960s. Alastair Morton died in 1963 and shortly after Morton Sundour was taken over by Courtaulds plc after which Edinburgh Weavers lost its pioneering and experimental edge.

Folly Cove Designers

Founded as a cooperative in Folly Cove, Lanesville, Gloucester, Massachusetts, by Virginia Lee Burton as a consequence of design courses she ran from 1938. Burton taught pattern design based on the principles of the nineteenth century Home Industries and Arts & Crafts Movements focusing on block-printing techniques. From 1940 students' work was exhibited and from 1943 those completing the course were able to submit a design which, if accepted by the jury of selected designers, was produced for sale under the Folly Cove name. The cooperative's production was marketed through America House of New York (established by the American Craftsmen's Cooperative Council) and the Home Industries Shop, Rockport, Massachusetts. By 1948 they also had their own summer retail unit in Folly Cove. In 1945 interest from the department store Lord & Taylor, who bought non-exclusive rights to five designs, raised the group's profile and led to increased publicity and new commissions. The group disbanded in 1970 after Burton's death the previous year.

Donald Hamilton Fraser
1929-2009

Born in London, Fraser, a painter, printmaker, writer and teacher trained initially as a journalist but after national service he studied at St Martin's School of Art, 1949-52, and in Paris 1953-54. Fraser worked mainly in oils and screen prints in the Scottish Colourist tradition, depicting ballet subjects and more abstract landscapes. He exhibited at Gimpel Fils from 1953 and Rosenberg, New York. He was influenced by de Staël, and the

School of Paris. Carel Weight took him on as a tutor and he was subsequently elected a fellow at the Royal College of Art (RCA) where he was involved 1957-83. Fraser designed at least two textiles for David Whitehead Ltd, at least one of which was exhibited at the 'Painting into Textiles' exhibition at the Institute of Contemporary Arts (ICA), 1953.

Fuller Fabrics Inc.
Established in New York in 1933 by Dan Fuller who personally oversaw the engagement of some of the most celebrated twentieth-century artists in the 'Modern Masters' range. Picasso was the first to be approached and was instrumental in obtaining introductions to Miró, Chagall and Léger as well as negotiating with Dufy's widow. Sixty patterns were produced in the range, including dress fabrics which were used by high profile designers, such as Claire McCardell and Tina Leser, and furnishing fabrics. The development of the company's 'Modern Masters' range involved a full year perfecting the printing technique to be used for production. The screen-printed furnishing fabrics were issued by Decorama, a division of Fullers, in 1956, the same year that designs by Braque and Klee were added to the range. Marketing was a key element of the launch of the range and involved a film outlining the production, booklets for sales staff and a travelling exhibition. The range appears to have been short-lived and by 1958 the company were focusing on their new 'Scanlandia' cottons. In the mid 1950s both Warhol and Rombola also designed a number of textiles for Fuller.

William Gear
1915-1997
Painter, printmaker, sculptor, curator and teacher, born in Methil, Fife, Scotland, Gear studied at Edinburgh College of Art and with Léger in Paris during 1937-8. He was involved in active service during the Second World War after which he returned to Paris for a time. Whilst serving in Germany he was able to secure the Berlin Art Collection at Schloss Celle and organised exhibitions of Modern Art that had been banned by the Nazi regime. In 1949 he held a joint exhibition with Jackson Pollock in New York. Gear was one of the first British artists to use screen-printing. He became curator of the Towner Art Gallery, Eastbourne 1958-64, and taught in Birmingham 1964-75. He exhibited at 'Painting into Textiles', 1953, and his paintings were translated into textile designs by Edinburgh Weavers and Horrockses. Gear also supplied designs to Sanderson & Son, and a range of

inexpensive woven fabrics for Dobson & M Browne & Co. His designs for wallpapers were executed by WPM Ltd.

Greef Fabrics Inc.
The American textile and wallpaper company was founded by Theodore Greef in 1933. Greef produced adaptations of traditional American floral prints and from the 1940s also developed a more contemporary range. The company introduced the concept of themed ranges in the early 1940s coordinating wallpapers and fabrics for interior decorators. Marion Dorn, Dan Rassmussen and Dagmar Wilson provided designs and, from 1952, they produced designs by the illustrator and artist Saul Steinberg. 'Opera' and 'Gendarmes' are amongst the designs Steinberg sold to Greef at this time. The company also had a successful business adapting vintage and traditional patterns. It was taken over by F Schumacher & Co in 1996, which relaunched Steinberg's designs from the Greef archive as fabrics and wallpapers in 2008. 'Trains' (which first appeared on the cover of *American Fabrics*, Spring 1950) and 'Aviary' were originally produced by Patterson but were reissued by Greef.

Lisa Grönwall
See Cliff Holden and the Marstrand Designers

Hammer Prints Ltd
The company was established by Eduardo and Freda Paolozzi and Nigel and Judith Henderson in 1954 to produce textiles, ceramics and furniture from their adjacent cottages in Essex. Although Paolozzi was already an established designer of fabrics and wallpapers, having taught textile design from 1949-54, many of the company's designs were worked and reworked by both Henderson and Paolozzi. They used images such as children's drawings, street hoardings, and natural and urban textures, and were very collaborative. Some of their earliest textile productions, such as 'Cloudburst' and 'Radar', date from pre-1957 and were not re-issued. Hammer Prints is probably best known for its furnishing fabrics that were printed and marketed through Hull Traders from 1957, including, 'Portabello', 'Barkcloth', 'Townscape', 'Paris Wall', 'Scrafitto', 'Coalface' and 'Cowcumber', and which were produced as wallpapers by Cole & Son. Paolozzi and Henderson also produced printed small runs of their designs on fabric for ties and scarves as well as producing bold, printed ceramic bowls and concrete furniture. But their methods of production proved too labour-intensive and the business closed down in 1961.

Merrick Hansel
b.1914
A painter, sculptor, poet and writer, born in Kent, Hansel's early work was mainly in mixed media; he produced mural decorations in the form of relief panels which became increasingly three-dimensional. His work was widely exhibited after the war including in a number of London shows. Two examples of his work were included in the 'Living Art Fabrics' exhibition by David Whitehead Ltd in 1969.

Anthony Harrison
b.1931
This painter and architect was born in Truro, Somerset. He studied architecture at the Northern Polytechnic, London from 1949; painting at Chelsea School of Art in 1951, and in 1952 spent time at the Central School of Arts and Crafts under Keith Vaughan. He was inspired by his travels, especially his regular visits to Spain, also Germany, France and Italy. His influences included Rembrandt, Goya, Turner, Monet and Klee. Harrison designed at least three textiles for Edinburgh Weavers.

Dennis Hawkins
1925- 2001
Painter, sculptor and printmaker, Hawkins studied at the Ruskin School of Drawing, Oxford, and at the Slade School, London, where he was taught by William Coldstream and Graham Sutherland. Hawkins exhibited at Gimpel Fils, the Redfern Gallery and with the London Group. He later became Head of Art at Repton School. Throughout the 1950s and 1960s he created reliefs, panels and murals for architectural projects and designed at least three screen-printed textiles for Edinburgh Weavers, including 'Bird Rose' and 'Blostma'.

Heal Fabrics Ltd
Founded 1941 as a subsidiary of the family furnishing company Heal & Son Ltd, which had been established in London in 1810, and originally called Heal's Wholesale & Export Ltd, Heal Fabrics was set up under the direction of Tom Worthington and Prudence Maufe to deal with the export of war surplus stock. However, the success of the textile ranges from 1944 led to the change of name in 1958 and a concentration on textile design under Worthington's influence. The early designs were typically small-scale printed patterns with limited colour printing in keeping with the war efforts. In the first ten years Worthington used the designs of more than seventy-five designers, many of whom were new graduates. Heal's shared a number of designers with their closest rivals, Hull Traders. In 1959 Heal's

introduced a range of roller prints and mechanised screen prints alongside the existing higher-priced hand screen-printed range. During the 1960s Heal's became increasingly important as a producer of avant-garde designs employing professional designers, in particular Lucienne Day and Barbara Brown, alongside artists such as Friedlinde de Colbertado Dinzl, John Plumb, Harold Cohen, Paule Vézelay, Haydon Williams, Cliff Holden, Maj Nilsson and Althea McNish. Heal's purchased a design from Zandra Rhodes' graduate show which was produced in the mid-1960s as 'Top Brass'. Tom Worthington's retirement in 1971 heralded the end of an era for Heal Fabrics, although the company continued to produce textiles into the 1980s.

John Heathcoat & Co.
Founded in 1808 by John Heathcoat (1783-1861) in Nottingham, but relocated to Devon in 1816. Originally concerned with lace making and bobbinet but by 1925 they had diversified into man-made fibres and cotton net. They supplied silk tulle for the wedding of Princess Elizabeth (later Queen Elizabeth II), and more recently Princess Diana, and during the 1940s and 1950s commissioned textile designs from artists such as Graham Sutherland and Gerald Wilde and the designer Jacqueline Groag. In 1969 the company sold 75% of its shares to Coats Paton Co. but a management buyout in 1984 put it back in the private hands of its directors and the Heathcoat-Amory family.

Nigel Henderson
1917-1985
Artist, designer, photo-collagist and teacher, born in London, Henderson studied biology at Chelsea Polytechnic, 1935-36. He was active in Group Theatre, worked for a period as a picture restorer and was encouraged by Peggy Guggenheim, with whom he became acquainted, to pursue his surrealist painting and collages. After active war service he suffered a nervous breakdown and began experimenting with photograms at the Slade School, London. He worked as a photo-journalist and designed posters for Ronnie Scott, the jazz impresario. Henderson was a close colleague of Paolozzi, with whom he travelled to Paris, and met Giacometti, Léger and Brancusi. Together they were instrumental in forming the Independent Group and, with their wives, set up Hammer Prints in Essex. Henderson organised the 'Parallel of Life and Art' exhibition, with Paolozzi and the Smithsons, at the Institute of Contemporary Art in 1953 and contributed to 'This is Tomorrow' at the Whitechapel Art Gallery in 1956. Henderson's first

major solo exhibition was held at the ICA in 1961. He collaborated with Paolozzi on many textiles for Hammer Prints Ltd, including 'Newsprint', which was produced as wallpaper by Cole & Son.

Barbara Hepworth
1903-1975
Sculptor and designer, born in Wakefield, Yorkshire, Hepworth studied at Leeds School of Art and the Royal College of Art, London. In 1925 Hepworth married the sculptor John Skeaping with whom she worked at the British School in Rome, Hepworth concentrating on marble carving. In 1933 she joined Abstraction-Création with her second husband, Ben Nicholson, and was given the impetus to carve pure geometric form. At the same time she and Nicholson exhibited eight hand block-printed textiles at Lefevre Gallery, some of which were later produced and sold through Nancy Nicholson's Poulk Press. Hepworth, Nicholson and Alastair Morton collaborated on a group of textiles for Edinburgh Weavers that were launched as part of the 'Constructivist' range in 1937. In 1939 they moved to St Ives, Cornwall, and set up an artists' colony with Naum Gabo. Hepworth designed ceramics for the 'Modern Art for the Table' exhibition at Harrods in 1934. She was commissioned to produce two works for the Festival of Britain in 1951 and during the 1950s worked on theatre sets for the Old Vic and Covent Garden. Porthia Textile Prints produced at least one design by Hepworth for a set of linen table mats in the late 1950s. These were printed by her assistant, and founder of the firm, Dennis Mitchell. She also designed a silk square for Ascher in 1947.

Patrick Heron
1920-1999
During 1937-9 Heron studied at the Slade School of Art. He was a conscientious objector during the war, spending his time farming near St Ives in Cornwall and, in 1944-45, working at Bernard Leach's Pottery in the town of St Ives, where he first met Hepworth and Nicholson. Heron was greatly influenced by Matisse's 'Red Studio', which he had seen at the Redfern Gallery in 1943. He taught for a time at the Central School of Arts & Crafts, London 1953-56. Heron began designing textiles for Cresta Silks Ltd, his father's company, at the age of fourteen and continued this through to the immediate post-war period. He designed at least six decorative, semi-figurative silk squares for Cresta, as well as fashion yardage, amongst which was 'Aztec', exhibited to some acclaim at 'Britain Can Make It' in 1946. Later decorative commissions

included a coloured glass window for the Tate St Ives, 1992, and a number of public projects. After the Second World War Heron developed an influential role as an art critic, writing for *New Statesman, Arts Digest*, *New York* and *Studio International*, and lecturing. In 1956 he turned to making abstract paintings and settled permanently in St Ives.

Cliff Holden
b.1919
Painter, designer, draughtsman, printmaker and teacher, born in Manchester, Holden originally studied agriculture, veterinary science, then philosophy, before studying painting under David Bomberg, Edna Mann and Dorothy Mead, whom he married. All these artists followed Bomberg to Borough Polytechnic and joined his group from the Bartlett School. Holden was a member of the London Group and a founder member, and briefly president, of the Borough Group in 1946. Holden settled in Sweden in the late 1950s where he set up a design studio with the painters Lisa Grönwall (with whom he had a child) and Maj Nilsson, known collectively as the Marstrand Designers. Holden was involved in promoting the work of Swedish painters and designers in Britain and vice versa. He taught in Sweden and at Goldsmiths' College, London. Holden, Nilsson and Grönwall designed fabrics for Hull Traders, Heal & Son, Edinburgh Weavers and David Whitehead Ltd and wallpapers for John Line and Lightbown Aspinall, a branch of WPM Ltd.

Horrockses Fashions Ltd.
Established 1946 as a division of Horrockses Crewdson & Co. Ltd, Preston (founded 1791), as a ready-to-wear fashion manufacturer. In the late 1940s James Cleveland Belle, the first director of the Cotton Board's Colour, Style and Design Centre, became the firm's design consultant and subsequently director. Belle was well acquainted with the leading British artists and had been the driving force behind many of the Centre's exhibitions including 'Designs for Textiles by 12 Fine Artists', which included work by Sutherland, Moore, Le Brocquy and Piper. Belle also knew Alastair Morton, who developed a working relationship with Horrockses after the war; supplying many designs for their printed cottons. Horrockses dresses were hugely successful and the firm prided itself on its high quality cloth, supplied by the parent company, and exclusive fabric designs. In 1953 Horrockses purchased paintings by Gear and Paolozzi, from the 'Painting into

Textiles' exhibition at the ICA, to produce as fabrics. Belle continued to look for new talent from the art colleges and in 1952 employed Pat Albeck on a part-time basis whilst she was still at the Royal College of Art; she remained with the firm until it was sold in 1958. Although the company's name existed until 1983, after the loss of Belle and Albeck in 1958 the firm never regained its prominence.

Jean Hugo
1894-1984
Painter, illustrator and theatre designer, and a great-grandson of Victor Hugo, Jean Hugo was acquainted with Cocteau and was also a relative of the jeweller François Hugo. He was born in Paris and grew up in an artistic environment surrounded by acclaimed artists working throughout his life in many media. From the 1920s onwards Hugo designed costumes and sets for the Ballets Suédois and later several artists' squares for Ascher.

Hull Traders Ltd
Founded in London by Tristram Hull in 1957, the company's design director was the Royal College of Art graduate Shirley Craven (b.1934) who joined the company in 1960 and became a director in 1963. Its strength was as a small firm with a highly experimental output. In 1961 it moved from London to Trawden, Lancashire. Hull Traders produced short runs of avant-garde furnishing fabrics, particularly large-scale abstract designs, winning several Design Centre Awards. Althea McNish, Trevor Coleman, Ivon and John Hitchens, Cliff Holden, Maj Nilsson, Robert Tierney, Susan Williams-Ellis, Friedlinde de Colbertado Dinzl and Humphrey Spender were amongst their artist designers, whose work, along with Craven's own designs, were produced under the title 'Time Present'. Hull Traders also marketed Hammer Prints Ltd's textiles in the late 1950s and absorbed the firm in 1961. During the 1960s Hull Traders produced some of the most radical textile designs of the era and in 1966 branched out into furniture design, including Bernard Holdaway's cardboard furniture. Hull Traders were taken over by Badehome Ltd in 1980, and dissolved in 1982.

Nevill Johnson
1911-1999
Painter and photographer, born in Derbyshire, England, Johnson moved to Ireland in 1934. Between 1934-1958 he worked in both Belfast and Dublin, exhibiting regularly with the Waddington Gallery, Dublin, from 1946 and at the influential 'Irish Exhibitions of Living Art', 1947-57, alongside Le Brocquy, Thurloe Conolly, and other

members of the White Stag Group [not to be confused with the US clothing company of the same name]. Johnson's early work was surrealist in nature but it was Picasso who he claimed as his only artistic hero and who was the later influence on his work. Johnson supplied two designs to John McGuire for Brown Thomas that were issued in 1953-1954: 'Mycycle' and 'Le Cirque'.

Elsbeth Juda
b.1911
Painter, collagist, photographer and teacher, Juda was born Elsbeth Goldstein in Darmstadt, Germany and lived and worked in Paris from 1929. She married Hans Juda in 1931 and moved to Berlin. In 1933 they fled Nazi Germany and settled in London. Elsbeth Juda studied photography with Lucia Moholy and worked for a time as a fashion photographer under the name 'Jay'. She became associate editor and photographer of *The Ambassador* magazine and was instrumental in persuading the textile industry to produce contemporary ranges. She founded 'Penthouse Studio' in 1963 with financial aid from ICI Fibres (for whom she worked as a consultant) to teach arts graduates industrial practice. Juda served on the Council of the Royal College of Art, London, and a number of other art school boards. She also painted and made large semi-autobiographical collages which have been exhibited in London, Germany and Switzerland.

Hans Juda
1904-1975
Journalist, editor and publisher, born Trier, Mosel, Germany, Juda married Elsbeth Goldstein, 1931. Whilst working in Berlin as the financial editor of *Berliner Tageblatt*. Hans and Elsbeth fled Nazi Germany, settling in London in 1933. Juda ran the London office of the journal *International Textiles* from 1934. In 1946, he relaunched the magazine as *The Ambassador* focusing on British exports. The magazine, which was immensely successful and influential, was taken over by Thomson Publications in 1964 and continued until 1972. The Judas collected contemporary art and became acquainted with many of Britain's leading artists and they commissioned many of them to produce illustrations and designs for the magazine. Juda conceived and organised the exhibition 'Painting into Textiles' in 1953, with his wife, Elsbeth, and Roland Penrose at the ICA. He served on the Council of the Royal College of Art, London and the board of the Central School of Arts and Crafts. He designed two printed textiles for Heal Fabrics Ltd in the 1960s.

Philippe Jullian
1919-1977
Illustrator, art critic, printmaker and writer; born Bordeaux, France, Jullian was an anglophile who split his time between Paris and London. He was born Philippe Simounet, taking his mother's maiden name aged eight, linking him to his distinguished historian grandfather Camille Jullian. Philippe Jullian was part of the Parisian 'Society' of which he was highly critical, publishing *Dictionnaire du Snobisme* (*Snob Spotter's Guide*) in 1958. He was a prolific writer collaborating on a number of books including works by Nancy Mitford, Angus Wilson and John Milner, as well as writing studies on Delacroix, Edward VII and, particularly, the Symbolist Movement. He illustrated many of his own books as well as classics such as Dickens, Wilde and Balzac. He designed artists' squares and printed dress fabrics for Ascher in the 1940s and designed a number of covers for *Vogue* in the late 1940s and 1950s.

Rockwell Kent
1882 -1971
American painter, printmaker, illustrator and political activist. In his youth Kent benefited from a long period of study and apprenticeship with various influential painters and theorists, amongst whom were William Merritt Chase, Arthur Wesley Dow and Kenneth Hayes Miller. From 1900-03, he studied architecture at Columbia University and between 1903-04 attended Robert Henri's classes at the New York School of Art. The following year he was apprenticed to Albert Thayer. His early paintings were first shown in New York in 1904 at the Society of American Artists, and his reputation as an early American Modernist was cemented when the Clausen Galleries showed his work in 1907. Some of his most celebrated work was for book illustration, and his 1930 three volume edition of *Moby Dick*, published by the Lakeside Press, is considered a masterpiece. He also illustrated *Beowulf*, the *Canterbury Tales* and the *Complete Works of Shakespeare*, and wrote and illustrated memoirs of various trips he'd made, including one to Alaska in 1918-19 and another there in 1920, and others to Tierra del Fuego & Greenland. During the 1920s, the 'Jazz Age', he produced witty and irreverent pen & ink drawings for *Vanity Fair*, the *New York Tribune*, *Harper's Weekly* and the original *Life* magazine. He also undertook a number of decorative interior projects, amongst which were a series of richly coloured reverse-glass paintings, exhibited at Wannamaker's Department Store in 1918, and murals for the interior

of the Cape Playhouse and Cinema, Cape Cod, in 1930, and another he designed in 1938 for the headquarters of the US Post Office in Washington DC. The Vernon Kilns Pottery, California, produced three different designs for tableware based on Kent's illustrations for 'Salamina', 'Our America' and 'Moby Dick'. He also designed nine furnishing textiles for Bloomcraft Inc, some of which – 'Palisades', 'Harvest Time', 'Deer Season', 'Waves of Grain' and 'Pine Tree'- were included by the company in their 1950 'Happily Married' range of textiles. Other applied work included the design of record sleeves and ceramic tiles. Kent was very active in leftwing politics, and in 1938 joined the International Workers Order (IWO), subsequently designing the organization's logo. In 1960 he gave several hundred of his paintings and drawings to the Soviet people, and in 1967, when awarded the Lenin Peace Prize , he donated the prize money equally to the women and children of both North and South Vietnam.

Laverne Originals
Laverne Originals, New York was founded in 1942 by husband and wife, Erwine and Estelle Laverne, to produce and promote well-designed Modernist objects. Estelle and Erwine were both members of the Art Students League where they met and began working together in 1934. Through the company they commissioned designs by leading artists, designers, architects and illustrators, including Alexander Calder, Willliam Katavolos, Oscar Niemeyer, Ray Komai, Alvin Lustig, Ross Littell and Douglas Kelley to sell in their stunning, Modernist showroom in New York.

Louis Le Brocquy
b.1916
Painter, printmaker, designer, born in Dublin, of Belgian descent, Le Brocquy studied chemistry at Trinity College, Dublin and worked in the family oil refining business in the 1930s. In 1938 he decided to take up painting full time. Largely self-taught, he worked in Dublin producing 'Tinker' paintings, stained glass and theatre designs and murals. In 1946 he moved to London exhibiting at Gimpel Fils and in 1948 produced his first tapestries for Edinburgh Tapestry Weavers. His interest in designing textiles developed and led to a number of commissions for tapestries and carpets. He also provided two textile designs to John McGuire, managing director of the upmarket retail store Brown Thomas, Dublin, 1953. Le Brocquy taught at the Central School of Arts and Crafts and was visiting tutor in textile design at the Royal College

of Art, London 1955-58, working alongside Margaret Leischner. He was a founding member of the Kilkenny Design Workshops, alongside Terence Conran, which he saw as an opportunity in Ireland to promote the integration of art and design as the Bauhaus designers had done. Following a trip to Spain with Jay (Elsbeth Juda) for *The Ambassador* in 1955 he designed the 'Iberia' range of textiles for David Whitehead Ltd and fashion textiles for Sekers and Horrockses Fashions. Le Brocquy designed a carpet for the exhibition 'Painters' Carpets' at the ICA in 1962. In 1954 Le Brocquy established the design consultancy Signa Ltd with the Irish architect Michael Scott.

Fernand Léger
1881-1955
Painter, sculptor and film-maker, born in Normandy, France, Léger initially trained as an architect's draughtsman. Having failed to gain a place at the École des Beaux-Arts, he studied at the École des Arts Décoratifs and the Académie Julian. Léger developed a form of cubist style painting often using strong colours. He spent the Second World War in the USA, and began painting large murals. In addition to his paintings; he created designs for sets and stage costumes, illustrated books, designed stained glass, sculptural polychrome ceramics and mosaics as well as tapestries. He established a ceramics studio at Biot, France in 1950. Maison Mybor produced several carpets designed by Léger, circa 1927. During the late 1950s he collaborated directly with Enrico Gregotti at the Italian firm of Bossi designing printed cotton textiles. Dan Fuller visited Léger to work on the production of a number of fabrics to his designs for Fuller's 'Modern Masters' range issued in 1955, the year of Léger's death.

Liberty & Co Ltd
Founded 1875 by Arthur Lasenby Liberty (1843-1917) as a warehouse for imported oriental goods in London, the company has a long history of commissioning designs from artists and architects. Liberty launched the subsidiary 'Young Liberty' in 1949 to sell contemporary post-war design in a controversial interior by Hulme Chadwick. In 1952 they held an exhibition of furniture, ceramics and fabrics by students of the Royal College of Art organised by Hugh Casson. Robert Stewart and Althea McNish were two of their regular designers and others included Martin Bradley and Pat Albeck. Liberty had a long-term relationship with Stewart, marketing his ceramics and hand-printed fabrics as well as commissioning a series of designs

for silk headsquares in the 1950s. Liberty printed its own fabrics at the Merton Abbey works until 1973.

Pádraig Macmiadhacháin
b.1929
Painter and printmaker, born in Downpatrick, Ireland, Macmiadhacháin studied at Belfast College of Art, National College of Art, Dublin, and the Academy of Art, Poland. Macmiadhacháin visited Moscow regularly and travelled extensively; he was inspired by magic markings and primitive religious objects, and the rich colours he saw on his travels. His paintings were largely abstract and semi-abstract oils and gouaches. David Whitehead Ltd chose three of his paintings to translate into fabrics for the ' Living Art Fabric' exhibition, 1969, including 'Dream City' and 'Sun God'.

Marino Marini
1901-1980
Sculptor, printmaker, painter, illustrator and teacher, born in Pistoia, Italy, Marini studied sculpture at the Accademia in Florence before moving to Paris at the age of eighteen, where he was influenced by the modern movements in art. He taught at Monza during the 1930s and at the Accademia Brera in Milan, 1940-70. In 1935 he won first prize for sculpture at Il Quadriennale, Rome. Throughout his career Marini was influenced by Etruscan and Roman art. He travelled throughout Europe and the United States exhibiting widely. He is best known for his equestrian subjects but he also executed a series of portraits of contemporaries including Stravinsky, Moore and Chagall. After 1942 Marini worked on illustrations for many books, a series of lithographs and graphic work and designed two textiles for Edinburgh Weavers.

Henri Matisse
1869-1954
Painter, sculptor, designer, collagist, teacher, illustrator, born in northern France, the son and grandson of weavers, Matisse originally studied law. During a prolonged period of illness he began drawing and decided to take up a career as an artist. He first exhibited his paintings at the salon de la Société Nationale des Beaux-Arts in 1896. Matisse studied sculpture in the late 1890s, although his first sculpture exhibition was not held until 1912, in New York. His work and that of his contemporaries, nicknamed 'Les Fauves', was controversial. He was a close associate of Picasso, exhibiting alongside him in 1918, and together the two had an enormous influence on modern art and design. Matisse had a natural talent for decorative

simplification, working with the bright colours he had seen on his travels in Africa and elsewhere. He designed a large frieze for the Paris 1900 World Fair, and also produced a large ceramic triptych, designed costumes and sets for ballets including Diaghilev's *The Nightingale* and completed illustrations for Mallarmé's *Poésies*. Whilst designing a Chinese emperor's cloak for Diaghilev he was based at Paul Poiret's studio in Paris. His work in the decorative arts included a limited edition carpet, 'Mimosa', produced by Alexander Smith & Sons circa 1950; a wallpaper, 'Abre en Fleur', for Katzenbach & Warren, 1948; silk squares and dress fabrics, as well as a pair of wall hangings based on cut-out shapes, inspired by his trip to Polynesia for Ascher in the late 1940s, the production of which he was closely involved in. The French firm Porthaud used a variation of the Ascher wall hanging design for bedlinen in the early 1950s.

John F McGuire
1929-2000
McGuire, considered an aesthete and purveyor of good taste, inherited Brown Thomas, the upmarket Dublin department store that had been bought by his grandfather, also John F McGuire, from Gordon Selfridge in 1933. The McGuire's had run a successful group of drapery stores based originally in Waterford since the mid-nineteenth century. In 1953 the younger John McGuire, commissioned a collection of hand-printed linens by four Modernist Irish artists, produced exclusively for Brown Thomas. The range included Louis Le Brocquy's 'Flight' and 'Megalithic'; Nevill Johnson's 'Mycycle' and 'Le Cirque'; 'Signum' by Thurloe Conolly and 'Irish Pubwall' by Patrick Scott. A selection of the textiles was exhibited at the Société des Artistes Decoratéurs, Grand Palais, Paris, in May 1954, and the Irish Design Exhibition, 1956.

Joan Miró
1893-1983
Born in Barcelona, Miró was a Catalan painter, sculptor and ceramicist. He studied art at La Escuela de la Lonja, under the landscapist Modesto Urgell y Inglada and José Pasco Merisa, the professor of decorative and applied arts. Towards the end of his life he increased the media in which he worked especially ceramics and his commissions included 'The Wall of the Moon' and 'The Wall of the Sun' at the UNESCO building in Paris. In 1974, after some initial reluctance, he created a tapestry for the World Trade Centre, New York, and having learnt the craft he went on to produced a number of other tapestries. Miró collaborated with Fuller Fabrics to produce a number of dress fabrics to his designs in 1955 having previously produced designs for a carpet, 'Spanish Dancer', for Maison Mybor, in the 1930s and a wallpaper for Katzenbach & Warren, 'El Sol', in 1948.

Henry Moore
1898-1986
Sculptor, draughtsman, artist and printmaker, born in Castleford, Yorkshire, Moore saw active service during World War I, and attended Leeds School of Art in 1919 and then the Royal College of Art, London. His early influences were the Egyptian, Greek and Etruscan rooms at the British Museum, the work of Picasso and a commitment to 'truth to material' which resulted in his direct carving techniques. In 1928 he held his first solo exhibition and received his first public commission for the London Underground Headquarters. In the 1930s he produced some figurative wall lights which were much admired by Paul Nash. During World War II he joined the War Artists' Scheme and his sketches were widely published. Moore was a prolific printmaker producing around seven hundred prints, mostly after 1955. He also designed a number of book covers and one of his drawings for 'Painting into Textiles' was used as the catalogue cover. He designed at least four scarves; dozens of printed dress fabrics for Ascher, of which around twenty were produced; at least four large printed wall hangings for Ascher which complemented those by Matisse, and two fabric designs produced by David Whitehead Ltd which were exhibited in 'Painting into Textiles'. Moore designed tapestries for Brose Partick, Black Isle and Ross & Cromarty in 1971 and, in 1976, the Tapestry Studio at West Dean College, Sussex created tapestries from his drawings that were exhibited at the Victoria and Albert Museum, London, in 1980.

Ben Nicholson
1894-1982
Painter, muralist, sculptor and designer, born in Denham, Buckinghamshire, Nicholson was the eldest son of the artists Sir William Nicholson and Mabel Pryde. He studied briefly at the Slade School, London, but suffered from ill health for much of his youth. In 1920 he married Winifred Dacre, with whom he collaborated to design rag rugs during the twenties. He held his first solo exhibition in 1924, at Gallery Twenty-one, and later exhibited with the London Group at Heal's Mansard Gallery. He married his second wife, Barbara Hepworth, in 1938. Nicholson co-edited the influential magazine *The Circle* with Naum Gabo. During the 1930s he was active in the applied arts creating rugs for Maison Mybor and a pile carpet, 'Project', made by Galerie Lucie Weill in association with Marie Culotti of Maison Mybor. Around 1931-3 he began designing a small number of hand-printed textiles for his own use and in 1934 exhibited six of them and four rugs, alongside Hepworth's designs, at Lefevre Gallery. These were printed from lino blocks and incorporated a reverse block as a 'signature' on each piece as well as a vertical or horizontal red line printed at intervals across the pattern. In the late 1930s he gave the blocks to his sister, Nancy Nicholson, who printed and retailed three designs from her shop, Poulk Press, in Motcomb Street, London in the 1940s. Nicholson exhibited designs for ceramics at 'Modern Art for the Table' in 1934 and in 1937 he produced six woven and printed designs for his friend Alastair Morton at Edinburgh Weavers, for the 'Constructivist' range. He designed ballet costumes and sets for Massine, but they were not used. Nicholson supplied further designs, such as 'Wasail', to Edinburgh Weavers in the 1950s, as well as a silk square design to Ascher in 1947. He also designed a panel for the Riverside Restaurant at the Festival of Britain in 1951 and a large mural for the Time Life Building in 1952. His graphic work included posters for Shell and Imperial Airways in the 1930s. He married his third wife, the photographer Felicitas Volger in 1957.

Roger Nicholson
1922-1986
Painter, designer and muralist, Nicholson was born in Australia, but moved to Kent, England as a child. He studied at Rochester School of Art and at the Royal College of Art under Gilbert Spencer until 1947. Nicholson taught at St Martin's School of Art for ten years and was Professor of Textile Design at the Royal College of Art 1958-84. His career as a textile designer was formidable. He worked for the Cotton Board as well as designing for David Whitehead Ltd, Sanderson's and Edinburgh Weavers. He was commissioned to produce two designs for Heal Fabrics, which, alongside Lucienne Day's 'Calyx', formed the focal point of the company's display at the Festival of Britain in 1951. He also designed wallpapers for Lightbown & Aspinall and WPM Ltd, lighting for Merchant Adventurers Ltd and completed murals for the Caledonian Hotel, Edinburgh, British Insurance Association and other clients.

Maj Nilsson
See Cliff Holden and the Marstrand Designers.

Michael O'Connell
1898-1976
Muralist, collagist and batik artist, O'Connell was born Dalton, Lancashire. A period studying at a seminary was followed by active service during the First World War. He spent time in Australia in the 1920s making pots, fonts and garden ornaments as well as painting. In 1937 he returned to England, married and settled in Hertfordshire. O'Connell perfected the use of batik and painting with dyes to create contemporary style wall hangings, which were used in Australia House and the Time Life Building, both in London, and other important interiors. He was also commissioned to create a huge hanging for the Country Pavilion at the Festival of Britain in 1951. His textile designs were influenced by primitive African, Australian and Polynesian art. He designed a block-printed velvet for Edinburgh Weavers in 1938, and during the 1940s and 1950s block prints and screen prints for Heal Fabrics Ltd.

Onondaga Silk Company
This New York textile manufacturer was founded in 1918 but had expanded by merging with Old Colony Silk Mills of New Bedford, Massachusetts by 1930. Their production included a wide range of dress fabrics including plain weaves, jacquards, velvets, printed rayons and silks. The company had previously collaborated with Raoul Dufy to produce a range of his designs for textiles from 1930 to1933. In late 1945 Onondaga were approached by Alan Gruskin, owner of Midtown Gallery, New York, to produce a range of printed textiles designed by a selected group of lesser-known artists, an idea mooted by his wife. Gruskin was keen to promote the commercial aspects of his artists' work and was very involved in the selection and development of the designs of these largely representational artists as well as the associated launch in December 1946. From the 55 paintings submitted Onondaga and Gruskin selected 22 paintings from six artists for the resultant 'American Artist Print Series'. The firm commissioned ready-to-wear designers to create garments from the fabrics for the launch, which were shown alongside the original paintings and fabric lengths and the range toured art museums and design schools throughout 1947-48. Onondaga continued tocollaborate with Gruskin, producing a second range in 1948, and also worked with Kennedy Galleries using images of birds in art in 1947.

John ('Jack') Packenham
b.1938
Packenham was a painter, poet, writer and teacher. Born in Dublin, he moved to Northern Ireland after his mother's death and graduated from Queen's University Belfast where he had studied French, Spanish and philosophy. Packenham lived in Ibiza for a time and in Dorset. He taught English in Belfast and had much of his poetry published. He was acquainted with Pádraig Macmiadhacháin who encouraged an interest in art and who taught him painting. He has exhibited in a number of solo and group shows including Group 63 between 1963 and 1973, and 'Art for Society' at the Whitechapel Art Gallery, 1978. Packenham designed three textiles for David Whitehead Ltd.

Eduardo Paolozzi
1924-2005
Sculptor, printmaker, collagist, textile designer and teacher, Paolozzi was born in Leith, Edinburgh, of Italian parents. He studied at Edinburgh College of Art and the Slade, London where he met William Turnbull, with whom he later shared a studio, and came into contact with Francis Bacon. He was influenced by Dada and the Surrealists and later by the writings of Wittgenstein and modern technology. Paolozzi's first solo exhibition was at the Mayor Gallery in 1947. Between 1947 and 1950 he worked in Paris where he met Giacometti. He designed a fountain for the Festival of Britain, 1951, and in 1956 took part in the Whitechapel Art Gallery's 'This is Tomorrow' exhibition. He founded the Independent Group with Nigel Henderson in 1952. Paolozzi taught textile design at the Central School of Arts & Crafts 1949-55, sculpture at St Martin's 1955-8 and, in 1968, was appointed lecturer in ceramics at the Royal College of Art. In 1951 he met and married Freda Elliot, a textile designer, and during the early 1950s Paolozzi began designing and hand screen-printing small quantities of fabrics. His collages, exhibited at 'Painting into Textiles', 1953, were produced as textiles by David Whitehead Ltd and Horrockses and in 1954 he set up Hammer Prints Ltd with Nigel Henderson. Their textiles and wallpapers, often collaboratively designed, were sold through Primavera and Hull Traders Ltd. Paolozzi was commissioned to decorate the offices of Ronald Jenkins at Ove Arup in 1952 where he worked with the Smithsons. In 1979 he designed a mosaic interior for Tottenham Court Road Underground Station, which was completed in 1985. He also designed an exhibition scheme for the Museum of Mankind, London and large bronze doors for the Hunterian Gallery, Glasgow. In 1970 he designed a ceramic decoration for Wedgwood that was produced as a limited edition series, and for Rosenthal AG, Germany. His 1972 plastic 'elephant' design to hold Nairn Floors Ltd's brochures in carpet and flooring retailers' outlets was produced in an edition of 3000. He also produced six designs for the Edinburgh Tapestry Company between 1967-80. Paolozzi was knighted in 1988 and awarded a KBE.

Patterson Fabrics and Piazza Prints
These companies were founded and run by Messrs Patterson and Piazza in New York and produced many furnishing fabrics and wallpapers to designs by Saul Steinberg, from 1947 until about the mid-1950s, and by John Rombola, from 1956 to 1968. Harben Papers, a subsidiary of Piazza Prints, also produced some of Rombola's designs under their name.

Francis Picabia
1879-1953
Painter, printmaker and writer, born in Paris, France, Picabia studied at the École des Beaux-Arts from 1897 and intermittently at the École des Arts Décoratifs. His earliest work was influenced by the Impressionist School and Sisley in particular, but after a trip to Spain he came into contact with Cubism and his work was exhibited alongside Gris, Léger and others in the Section d'Or. Picabia spent the First World War in New York where he was influenced by modern American art and his work became dominated by the importance of the machine in the modern world. He used 'found' objects to create mixed media collages during the 1920s and was an influential figure in the Dada movement. Picabia also designed costumes, sets and decoration for a number of ballets and published his poems. He was commissioned to design a silk square, 'Sans Bourne', for Ascher in 1947.

Pablo Picasso
1881-1973
Painter, sculptor, designer, writer and printmaker, born in Malaga, Spain, he studied at the Barcelona Art School. At nineteen he went to Paris to paint. Picasso was hugely influenced by primitive art and developed this into Cubism. He was very experimental with his methods and techniques, and was one of the first artists to make sculpture from 'found' objects. His style and work changed significantly over the years and from medium to medium. He was encouraged by Cocteau to make designs for the ballet *Parade* with music by Eric Satie which introduced him to a new circle of friends around Diaghilev. In 1928 he designed the first of a series of carpets for Maison Mybor, which was woven in Algeria. From the 1930s he wrote poetry and books and a play, *Desire Caught by the Tail*. His ceramics, made at the Madoura Pottery, Vallauris, in the south of France, 1946-69, initially used traditional shapes but later he experimented with zoomorphic shapes, new glazes and sgraffito. Replicas or copies made from moulds were sold in limited editions. He produced designs for silver plates and jewellery made by François Hugo. He designed a silk scarf for the ICA in 1950 and another screen-printed scarf to raise funds for the peace movement in 1951. Fashion fabrics designed by him for Fuller Fabrics were used by the American fashion designer Claire McCardell in 1954, and a number of furnishing cottons were produced to his designs by Bloomcraft in 1963. That same year the American sportswear manufacturer White Stag collaborated with him to produce fabrics to his designs for an exclusive range of apres-ski wear.

John Piper
1903-1992
Painter, illustrator, poet, writer and designer, born in Epsom, Surrey. Following the death of his father in 1926 Piper studied at Richmond School of Art and the Royal College of Art, London. During the 1930s he worked as an art critic. He was involved with Abstraction-Création in 1934, and a member of the Seven and Five Society and the London Group. In the 1940s he was associated with the neo-Romantics and his collages and paintings were influenced by English architecture and topography. Piper helped John Betjeman edit the Shell Guides and, during World War II, joined the War Artists' Scheme. He designed sets and costumes for the theatre in the 1930s and 1940s including Britten's *Rape of Lucretia* at Glyndebourne. Piper designed many book illustrations and covers including several for *International Textiles*, later known as *The Ambassador*. His stained glass designs were used at Eton College Chapel and Coventry Cathedral, amongst others, and he also designed glass for Steuben, USA, for an exhibition 'Design in Glass by 27 Contemporary Artists', 1940. His first tapestry for Chichester Cathedral, 1965-6, led to at least fourteen further tapestry commissions as well as a series of editioned tapestries executed by a number of companies including Pinton Frères, Aubusson, the Edinburgh Tapestry Company and Ibenstein Weavers, Namibia. He designed tables with mosaic tops made by Dennis M Williams, Kingston upon Thames, between 1958 and 1961. Piper also produced designs for ceramics in 1972, in collaboration with Geoffrey Eastop, and in 1982 with the Fulham Pottery. In 1947, Piper, along with many other artists supplied designs for Ascher Ltd's headsquares. 'Medieval Head' was produced but two other designs that may have been intended for use were not issued; nor was a large mural panel which was discussed but appears not to have been taken beyond the discussion stage. David Whitehead Ltd used several paintings by Piper from 'Painting into Textiles', 1953, three of which were screen-printed onto cotton by autumn 1954 and they included four of his textiles in their 'Living Art Fabrics' exhibition, 1969; in all Piper supplied Whitehead with at least twelve designs. Piper also produced five designs for textiles for Sanderson's centenary in 1960 and a silk square for Ascher in the 1940s.

John Plumb
1927-2008
A painter and teacher, Plumb was born in Luton, Bedfordshire. He served an apprenticeship at Vauxhall Motors as well as studying at Luton School of Art, the Byam Shaw School and the Central School of Art and Design, London, where he was taught by Anthony Gross, Victor Pasmore, William Turnbull and Keith Vaughan. He held his first one-man exhibition in 1957 at Gallery One, London. In 1960 he exhibited alongside William Turnbull and Bridget Riley in the 'Situation' exhibition. Plumb taught at a number of schools in England and America, including the Central School 1969-82, and exhibited widely in the UK and abroad. His earlier work was strictly abstract, often incorporating mixed media, but during the 1970s he worked on more figurative paintings. He designed a printed furnishing fabric for Heal Fabrics and a carpet design for the 'Painter's Carpets' exhibition at the ICA, 1962.

Ruth Reeves
1892-1966
American painter, textile designer, graphic designer and academic. After attending the California School of Design, San Francisco, Reeves went to New York in 1911, where she continued her studies at the Pratt Institute, Brooklyn, winning an Art League scholarship in 1913. Having finished her academic studies she worked as a batik artist and then for the magazine, *Women's Wear Daily*. In 1920 she travelled to Paris to study art at the Academie Moderne under Fernand Léger. Following her return to New York in 1928, she became design consultant to W & J Sloane's furniture store, and the

company exhibited a group of twelve textiles she had designed for them at the Third International Exhibition of Contemporary Industrial Art, held by the American Federation of Arts at New York's Metropolitan Museum of Art in 1930/31. Amongst these was her iconic printed cotton textile 'Manhattan'. Between 1930/33 she was a member of the American Union of Decorative Artists and Craftsmen, and in 1932, received one of her most important commissions from the industrial and interior designer Donald Deskey, to create textile, carpet & wallpaper designs for New York's newly built Radio City Hall, including a tapestry and carpet for the grand foyer. Her 'Hudson River' series of textiles of 1933 gained her a fellowship grant from the Gardiner School Alumni Foundation, and in 1934 she received a Carnegie Travelling fellowship, which enabled her to visit Guatemala, an event which had a significant and lasting influence on the future direction of her career. Her trip to Guatemala resulted in 'Adaptations' – an exhibition of her textiles inspired by her researches there, held in New York in 1935, which included the important textile 'Guatemalan Document'. This and four others of her Guatemalan influenced textiles were produced commercially by Reeves for retailing by the department store R H Macy & Co. In 1936 she was appointed National Coordinator of the Index of American Design – a considerable academic undertaking – and she subsequently expanded her researches to include the textiles of Ecuador, Peru and Bolivia, receiving a Guggenheim fellowship in 1940 to facilitate these. In 1956 she travelled to India, having been awarded a Fulbright Fellowship to study there, and was appointed by the Indian government Advisor in Handicrafts to the Register General of India, for whom she documented craft traditions. Despite the additional pressure of these many undertakings she continued to create commercial designs, producing an highly innovative scarf design for the New York World Fair in 1939 and, in the later 1940s, working with the distinguished British printmaker Stanley William Hayter, designing scarves and ties for a New York based artist's cooperative 'Contempora Etched Originals'. Throughout the 1950s she designed not only textiles, but also a wide variety of domestic objects, amongst which were ceramic tiles, melamine trays and a variety of greetings cards.

Alan Reynolds
b.1926
Born in Newmarket, Suffolk, Reynolds was a painter and teacher. After active service in World War II he studied at Woolwich Polytechnic. He exhibited with the London Group in 1950 and held his first solo exhibition at the Redfern Gallery in 1952. He later exhibited widely in Europe and America. Reynolds taught at the Central School of Art and Design and St Martin's. He was very influenced by the work and writings of Paul Klee. His early paintings often used nature as a theme, albeit in a semi-abstract way. Later he moved towards pure abstract painting and began making constructions and reliefs. Reynolds designed several furnishing fabrics for Edinburgh Weavers and a tapestry for Clydesdale Bank made by Edinburgh Tapestry Company's Dovecot Studio in 1964.

Zandra Rhodes
b.1940
Textile designer, fashion designer and painter, born in Chatham, Kent, Rhodes studied at Medway College of Art and the Royal College of Art, London. Heal Fabrics Ltd purchased a design from her degree show in 1964 which they produced as a furnishing fabric, 'Top Brass' and, in 1966, a further design from the degree show, 'Stalactite', was produced as a black and white printed textile. WPM Ltd produced a wallpaper to Rhodes' design for Crown's 'Palladio' range in 1968 and Sanderson's produced a wallpaper by her circa 1965. Rhodes initially set up a print studio with Alex McIntyre, hand screen-printing and selling her textiles direct to fashion houses such as Foale & Tuffin. She then went into partnership with Sylvia Ayton who began producing clothes using Rhodes' textiles which they sold through the Fulham Road Clothes Shop and her own shop in Grafton Street, London.

John Rombola
b.1933
An American artist and illustrator, Rombola's earliest designs were illustrations for *Fashion and Travel* magazine, 1954. He was also commissioned to provide illustrations for *Life*, *Town & Country*, *Horizon*, *New York Herald Tribune* and *Holiday* and designed a number of record covers and posters. During the fifties Rombola supplied designs for fabrics to Arundell Clarke and Fuller Fabrics. From 1956-68, he supplied designs for textiles and wallpapers to Piazza Prints, and its subsidiaries Patterson Fabrics and Harden Papers, including a psychedelic version of 'Alice in Wonderland'. His first one-man exhibition was at the D'Arcy Gallery, New York, in 1961. Rombola

has published three books and has designed stage sets and costumes for the Harkness Ballet Company. For the launch of the book *John Rombola, Eclectic Eccentric*, in 2010, he was commissioned to design five window displays for the New York Fifth Avenue department store, Bergdorf Goodman.

Ben Rose
1916-2004
Born in Indiana, Rose studied at the Art Institute of Chicago, University of Chicago and De Paul University. After serving four years in the US Navy he set up his design studio in 1946, producing textile and wallpapers hand-printed from the same screens, following a one-off commission from an architect friend. That same year he won his first design award. From 1947 he collaborated with the interior designer Helen Stern. Rose's designs were a favourite of Modernist architects and the studio grew rapidly, reaching around fifty employees by 1967. A widely exhibited and successful designer, he was given three design awards by the American Institute of Decorators, 1952. His textile designs were produced by his own company, Ben Rose, Inc. and were distributed by L Anton Maix and through his own showroom in the Chicago Merchandise Mart.

Kenneth Rowntree
1915-1997
Painter, collagist illustrator, muralist, draughtsman and teacher, born in Scarborough, Yorkshire, Rowntree studied at the Ruskin School then the Slade School with Randolph Schawbe. He taught at the Royal College of Art, the Ruskin School and the University of Newcastle. He was an official war artist and participated in the 'Recording Britain' project. He held his first solo exhibition at the Leicester Galleries in 1946. Rowntree was involved in illustrating the King Penguin series of books in 1947 and designed a lithographic print for the Baynard Press School Prints series, which was exhibited at the Festival of Britain, 1951. He created a number of murals, including one for the British Pavilion at the Brussels International Exhibition in 1958, and was a member of the Society of Mural Painters from the early 1940s. His work is often related to structure and pattern as landscapes, townscapes or semi-abstract collages. Rowntree designed a number of furnishing fabrics for Edinburgh Weavers.

Sanderson, Arthur & Sons Ltd.
Founded in 1860, in Uxbridge Middlesex, as an importer and then manufacturer of wallpapers by Arthur Sanderson (d.1882), it only began producing printed textiles in

1921 and woven textiles after 1934. The textile branch of the company was originally known as Eton Rural Cretonnes and later as Eton Rural Fabrics. They had a large in-house design studio but also commissioned artists such as Douglas Cipriani, and Humphrey Spender who produced several designs for the company. Edward Bawden designed both fabrics and wallpapers for them. In 1960, to celebrate their centenary, Sanderson's commissioned a special series of designs for textiles and papers from a number of influential artists including John Piper, Raymond Loewy, Jacqueline Groag, Gio Ponti and Frank Lloyd Wright. From 1951 the company also marketed and distributed foreign manufacturers' textiles exclusively in the UK, including those by Stig Lindberg, Gio Ponti, Ken Scott and Frank Lloyd Wright as well as Picasso's designs for Bloomcraft. Over the many years since its establishment Sanderson has merged with and been involved in many takeovers, most recently by Walker Greenbank plc, and continues producing both traditional and modern wallpapers, paints and textiles.

Schiffer Prints
Founded by Milton Schiffer in 1945, as a division of Mil-Art Co. Inc. Schiffer's first 'Stimulus Collection' of printed fabrics, including designs by six architects, artists and designers, was launched in 1949. It contained five designs by Salvador Dalí as well as designs by Ray Eames, Abel Sorenson, Edward J Wormley, Bernard Rudofsky and George Nelson. A number of the designs were later also produced as wallpapers. The New York Times described the 'Stimulus Collection' as 'Unquestionably the most brilliant single collection of all modern prints introduced since the war'.

William Scott
1913-1989
Painter, printmaker, sculptor and teacher, Scott was born in Greenock, Renfrewshire, but moved to Enniskillen, Northern Ireland, as a child and studied at Belfast College of Art and the Royal Academy Schools, London. During the 1930s he spent time working in Cornwall, France and Dublin. He served in the Ordnance Section of the Royal Engineers during World War II, during which time he produced watercolour landscapes and learnt lithography. He met Henry Cliffe during the war and after it spent time teaching at Corsham. In Cornwall Scott became acquainted with Lanyon, Nicholson, Wynter and Frost. His first solo exhibition was held at the Léger

Gallery in 1942. During the 1950s he met with Pollock, de Kooning, Rothko and Kline in America. Scott's mural for Altnagelvin Hospital, 1958-61, won him first prize in the John Moore's Liverpool exhibition in 1959. He taught painting in a number of art schools in England, Germany and Canada. A number of Scott's paintings were successfully translated into both woven and printed furnishing fabrics by Alistair Morton for Edinburgh Weavers, including his painting 'Nearing Circles'; a drawing for 'Skaill' and a sketch for 'Skara Brae'. Scott had a painting included in the ICA's 1953 exhibition 'Painting into Textiles', which was subsequently produced as a textile by David Whitehead Ltd. He also designed a carpet for the exhibition of 'Painters' Carpets', also held at the ICA, London, in 1962. He produced lithographic illustrations for Frederick Muller's *Soldiers' Verse* and Camden Classics *Jane Eyre*.

Sekers (West Cumberland Silk Mills) Ltd

The company was founded in 1938 by Hungarian Miki Sekers and his cousin Tommy de Gara, in Whitehaven, Cumbria, using a government grant to produce fashion silks. After the war the firm returned to the production of fashion fabrics and supplied many of the leading couturiers including Edward Molyneux, Christian Dior, Pierre Balmain, Victor Stiebel, Hardy Amies, Norman Hartnell, Digby Morton, Givenchy and Balenciaga. They supplied the fabrics for a number of the Royal Family's outfits including Princess Margaret's wedding dress. Oliver Messel, who had helped Miki Sekers design and build the Rosehill Theatre in his garden, supplied designs to the firm alongside Cecil Beaton, Graham Sutherland and Louis Le Brocquy. Sekers purchased a Jon Catleugh painting from the 'Painting into Textiles' exhibition at the ICA, 1953, which was translated into a printed silk. Nine of Sekers' fabrics, alongside their original designs, were included in an exhibition 'Modern Art in Textile Design' at the Whitworth Gallery, Manchester in 1962; 'Lady Sylvia' and 'Rose Bouquet' by Cecil Beaton; 'Nosegay', 'Tulips', 'Avernus' and 'Carnation' by Oliver Messel; and 'Lattice', 'Shepherd' ('Blown Rose') and 'Stoney' ('Night Flowers') by Graham Sutherland. From 1960 Sekers developed a silk and rayon mix furnishing fabric, which won the Duke of Edinburgh's Council of Industrial Design Award for Elegant Design in 1962. Today the firm is known as Sekers Fabrics and concentrates exclusively on the production of furnishing fabrics, which it began during the 1960s.

Wesley Simpson Custom Fabrics, Inc.

Wesley Simpson founded his eponymous company in New York in 1933 to produce dress fabrics for the home dressmaking market as well as for American fashion houses. A salesman by trade, he had various marketing strategies to ensure his fabrics reached the widest possible audience. He used an 'exclusivity' strategy, granting only one store in each town or city rights to sell his moderately priced over-the-counter fabrics. He also supplied a line of couture fabrics to the design houses and by the early 1940s the firm included some of the more distinguished New York garment houses, including Townley Frocks, whose designer was Clare McCardell, among their clients. The company made a concerted effort to expose its name and products to the American market in the immediate post-war period. Marcel Vertes was a prolific designer supplying more than 60 textiles, and 6 scarves to his designs were produced in the period 1942-48. In 1946 the 'Wesley Simpson Artists Series' launched their involvement with Salvador Dalí and included six textiles and nine scarves. Simpson also bought designs from Ludwig Bemelmans, illustrator of the 'Madeline' books, which were included in their 'Museum Prints' collection.

Edward Steichen
1879 -1973

American photographer, painter, art gallery & museum curator. Edward Steichen was just a year old when he moved with his family from Luxembourg to the United States in 1880. At the age of fifteen, in 1894, he began a four year lithography apprenticeship with the Milwaukee American Fine Art Company. While developing his drawing skills there he taught himself to paint in his spare time, and it was also then that he first became interested in photography. In 1900 he was introduced to the pioneering photographer, modern art promoter and gallery owner, Alfred Steiglitz, with whom he formed a long lasting friendship and, subsequently a business partnership. In 1902 he designed the logo and typeface for Steiglitz's magazine *Camera Works*, and became the most regularly featured photographer in this influential publication. He also collaborated with Steiglitz to open the gallery 'The Little Galleries of the Photo-Succession', on New York's Fifth Avenue, later known as '291', which exhibited not only photography, but also work by modern European artists such as Matisse, Picasso, Rodin and Brancusi. Steichen is considered to have created the first true modern fashion photography when he photographed gowns by the radical French couturier Paul Poiret in 1911, for publication in *Art et Decoration*. The Stehli Silks Corporation commissioned textile designs from Steichen in 1926 for their textile range of 'Americana Prints'. His designs were derived from dramatically-lit Surrealist photographic close-ups of everyday objects, such as rice, sugar lumps, mothballs, matches, carpet tacks and eye glasses. In the later 1930s he also collaborated with Mallinson Fabric's on a textile collection called 'Camera Prints'. In the 1920s and 1930s he worked extensively for Condé Nast, his photography being published mainly in *Vogue* and *Vanity Fair*, whilst concurrently working for leading advertising agencies such as J. Walter Thompson, all of which resulted in his becoming one of the best known and most highly paid photographers of the era. During the Second World War he commanded the Naval Aviation Photographic Unit, and his propaganda documentary, *The Fighting Lady*, won a 1945 Academy Award for best documentary. Following the war he was appointed Director of the Department of Photography at the Museum Of Modern Art in New York, where, in 1955, he was curator of the ground breaking photographic exhibition, *The Family of Man*, which travelled to sixty-nine different countries, and was seen by nine million people. He retired from the Museum in 1962, and in 1963 was awarded the Presidential Medal of Freedom.

Saul Steinberg
1914-1999

Romanian-born American artist, cartoonist, satirical illustrator and sculptor, best known for his work for the *New Yorker* for whom he worked for nearly 60 years. Steinberg initially trained as an architect in Italy where he perfected his line drawing and began publishing cartoons in the satirical magazine *Bartoldo*. By the 1940s his work was published in *Harper's Bazaar* and *Life* but in 1941 he fled fascist Italy for USA when he began working for the *New Yorker*. Throughout his life a number of books of his drawings have been published. Steinberg held his first one-man show at the Wakefield Gallery, New York, in 1943. After the war he became a travelling ambassador for American art and exhibited all around Europe including, ICA, London, in 1952; the 1954 Milan Triennale; and in 1958 the Brussels World's Fair. During the 1970s he experimented with sculpture. Many of his drawings were adapted into textiles, in particular border prints, and wallpapers by companies such as Greef Fabrics, Piazza Prints and their furnishing fabrics subsidiary, Patterson Fabrics, from the mid-1940s to mid-1950s. Correspondence in the Steinberg Foundation suggests he was also discussing designs for fashion yardage with Stehli Silks but there is no evidence that these were produced. A further series of roller-printed, cotton border prints exist with Steinberg designs but it has not been possible to attribute these to a manufacturer at this time. A silk headsquare for the French company, Maison Brochier, Lyons, was produced to his design in 1966.

Robert Stewart
1924-1995

Textile, ceramic and graphic designer, painter and teacher, Stewart spent most of his life in Glasgow and studied at the Glasgow School of Art, 1942-47. From 1949 he worked in the school's printed textile department, becoming Head of Department, Head of Design and later the school's Director, retiring in 1984. Throughout his teaching he remained a dynamic and innovative force pushing his students and the department into new areas. His first commission in 1949 was for furnishing textiles for John Noble, Ardkinglass, and by the following year he had made contact with Liberty of London for whom he was to work for the next 15 years or more. He was principal designer for Liberty in the 1950s producing textiles, scarves and graphic designs used on ceramics and other household goods for their 'Young Liberty' label launched in 1949. He sold six designs to Morton Sundour in 1950, began work on an embroidery project for the Festival of Britain and his two tapestry designs for Dovecot Tapestries were exhibited at the Saltire Society's Edinburgh Festival show the same year. Stewart also ran a small workshop (Robert Stewart Ceramics Ltd) producing his own screen-printed ceramics (1957-63) that were marketed through Liberty and Primavera. He designed ceramic tiles, table mats, greetings cards, wrapping papers and posters for Edinburgh Tapestry Company (1951-6) alongside tapestries and textiles for Donald Brothers. During his teaching he worked with ICI and Pringle in the development of new techniques in textile printing and fashion design. He received a number of prestigious commissions for ceramic mural panels in public buildings throughout the UK. During the late 1960s and throughout the 1970s he began exhibiting his paintings and held a number of solo shows.

Graham Sutherland
1903-1980

Print-maker, painter, designer, illustrator and teacher, Sutherland was born in London and educated at Epsom College, Surrey. He began an engineering apprenticeship in Derby, followed by a period at Goldsmiths College, London, studying etching. His principal inspiration in these early prints was the revival of interest in the work of Samuel Palmer and he taught etching at Chelsea 1926-35. He held his first solo exhibition in 1925 at Rosenberg & Helft. However, after the Wall Street Crash in 1929 and the collapse of the print market, Sutherland turned to design, teaching and painting. He exhibited with the London Group from 1936-37 and served as a war artist from 1941-44. Sutherland produced tableware designs for E Brain & Co, and A J Wilkinson Ltd that were exhibited at 'Modern Art for the Table', Harrods, London, 1934. His glass for Stuart & Sons was exhibited at 'British Art in Industry' at the Royal Society of Arts, 1935. He produced glass designs for Steuben, USA in 1940, wallpapers for Cole & Son Ltd and machine woven carpets for Carpet Trades Ltd, Kidderminster. Sutherland received the commission for the altar tapestry for the new Coventry Cathedral in 1951. After ten years' work the monumental 'Christ in Glory', woven by Pinton Fréres, France, was unveiled in 1962, although in the meantime the Edinburgh Tapestry Company had worked up several smaller variations, and other designs by Sutherland, into finished pieces. He began designing printed textiles during the late 1930s, exhibiting in the Cotton Board's 'Designs for Textiles by Fine Artists' alongside Piper and Wilde in 1941, and continued throughout the 1940s and1950s working for S W Whaley & Son Ltd; H Ledgard Ltd; T & A Wardle & Son Ltd; Horrockses Fashions Ltd; Helios Ltd; West Cumberland Mill Silks (later Sekers); Cresta Silks Ltd; Warner & Sons and Ascher. A close friend of the Judas', Sutherland's work was enthusiastically published and promoted by the *Ambassador*.

Angelo Testa
1921-1984

A painter and sculptor, born in Springfield, Massachusetts, USA, Testa studied at the New York School of Fine and Applied Arts, the University of Chicago and became the first graduate of the New Bauhaus, Chicago, under Gyorgy Kepes, Marli Ehrmann, László Moholy-Nagy and George Fred Keck. He is acknowledged as a pioneering and influential textile designer in the USA introducing abstract motifs into commercial textile design. His firm, Angelo Testa Fabrics, which he set up to produce hand-printed textiles in 1947, produced many of his designs. He soon began producing woven textiles and, by winning large contracts, was able to finance the opening of a shop. Testa supplied textile designs on a freelance basis to Cohama (Cohn-Hall-Marx), Forster, Greef, Knoll (from 1945) and Schumacher. He also designed paper napkins, place mats and printed wall hangings. Testa received four 'Good Design' awards, between 1950-55, from the Museum of Modern Art, New York. In the 1970s he experimented with rug designs and produced a huge metal sculpture for Peerless, a Chicago sweet manufacturer.

Robert Tierney
1936-2008

An artist and designer who studied at Plymouth College of Art, 1955-58, and with Alan Reynolds at the Central School, Tierney exhibited widely in London and abroad. He designed textiles for David Whitehead Ltd, F W Grafton & Co Ltd, Fidelis Furnishing Fabrics, Edinburgh Weavers and Hull Traders Ltd.

Joe Tilson
b.1928

Painter, sculptor and printmaker, Tilson was born in London. He worked as a carpenter and joiner during 1944-46, served in the RAF 1946-49, and studied at St Martin's School of Art and the Royal College of Art 1952-55 alongside Peter Blake, Bridget Riley and Richard Smith. His Rome Prize from the RCA took him to Italy and Spain; travels that influenced his early work. However, after seeing the Abstract Expressionist exhibition in 1956, his work became more abstract and in the late 1950s he began producing geometric wood reliefs. His first one-man show was at the Marlborough Gallery in 1962. During the 1960s he increasingly used screen-printing and multiples often incorporating contemporary events and political figures. Tilson was associated with the Pop Art movement and in particular the work of Peter Phillips. He designed fabrics for Edinburgh Weavers and produced a carpet design for the "Painters' Carpets" exhibition at the ICA, 1962.

Feliks Topolski
1907-1989

Painter, draughtsman, muralist and illustrator, born in Warsaw, Poland, Topolski Studied at the Academy of Fine Art, Warsaw, 1925-30, as well as in Paris and Italy. Topolski came to England in 1935, to record the Silver Jubilee of George V for a Polish magazine but decided to stay. During the Second World War he was an officer in the Polish Army and served as a war artist for both the Polish and British governments, becoming a British subject in 1947. Topolski designed theatrical costume and sets, TV sets and numerous book and periodical illustrations. He also made films for BBC TV and published his wartime sketchbooks. *Topolski's Chronicles* were published fortnightly, almost continuously, 1953-1979, illustrating the major events of the world through his distinctive pencil and pen sketches. Two important mural commissions included 'Cavalcade of the Commonwealth' for the Festival of Britain, in 1951, and 'Coronation of Elizabeth II' at Buckingham Palace. Ascher produced some of his first silk squares from Topolski's wartime sketchbooks, circa 1945, as well as dress fabrics to his designs. Jacqmar also produced a scarf to Topolski's design.

Victor Vasarely
1908-1997

Painter, writer and designer, born in Pécs, Hungary, Vaserley studied at the State School, Academy of Painting, Budapest, and the Bauhaus 1929-30. His first solo show was held in Budapest in 1930 and the same year he moved to Paris, married and began working as a commercial artist. He turned back to painting in 1944, began writing in the 1950s and made two films in the 1960s. From an early stage his work was concerned with illusions of space and connected with the schools of Orphism and Surrealism. His interest in simple line and profile and the use of colour in decoration stemmed from his Bauhaus training. He exhibited at 'Aubusson Tapestries by 12 Abstract Artists' in New York, 1952. At least two designs by Vasarely were produced by Edinburgh Weavers, one printed, one woven. Vasarely also designed rugs and tapestries as well as ceramics for Rosenthal AG, Germany.

Keith Vaughan
1912-1977

Painter, draughtsman, diarist and teacher, Vaughan was born in Selsey Bill, Sussex, educated at Christ's Hospital and worked for Lintas Advertising Agency. He painted part-time until the war, when, as a conscientious objector he spent a year at Shere. He served in the Pioneer Corps and worked as a German interpreter for prisoners of war in Yorkshire. At this time he came into contact with Graham Sutherland, John Craxton, Robert Colquhoun and John Minton. His first solo show of drawings was at the Lefevre Gallery, London, in 1942. He taught at Camberwell School of Arts and Crafts, the Central School of Arts and Crafts and the Slade School of Fine Art, London. Vaughan kept journals which were published during and after his lifetime. In 1951 he was commissioned to paint a mural for the Festival of Britain's Dome of Discovery. He designed several textiles for Edinburgh Weavers, one of which, 'Adam', won the Design Centre Award for Textiles in 1958.

Marcel Vertes
1895-1961

Hungarian Painter, illustrator, author, muralist, ceramicist, textile and costume designer. Born in Budapest. After serving in the First World War, Vertes abandoned his law studies and gravitated to Paris to become an artist, in order, he said provocatively in an interview with *Vogue*, 'to paint women in the nude'. From the 1930s onwards he produced covers and illustrations for, amongst many others, *Vogue*, *Harpers Bazaar*, and *Graphis*. He also began a long working association in the 1930s with the Surrealist couturier Elsa Schiaparelli, for whom he designed many advertisements and promotional illustrations. He undertook other graphic work for Kayser Hosiery, Rosemary de Paris, Candy and Antoine de Paris cosmetics. Discharged from active service in the Second World War, he left France for the United States in 1940, where he set up a studio in New York on West 57th St. In the 1940s he designed at least six scarves and over sixty fashion fabrics for the New York textile manufacturer Wesley Simpson Custom Fabrics Inc. Whilst in the States he illustrated books by Ernest Hemmingway, executed murals for the Cafe of the Carlyle Hotel in New York, and, in the 1950s, designed ceramic decorations for Castleton China, New Castle, PA. In 1952 he won two Academy Awards for the art direction and costume design of the musical film, *Moulin Rouge*. In the mid 1950s he returned to live in Paris, and from 1955, until his death in 1961, designed ceramics for Les Ateliers du Tapis Vert in the southern French town of Vallauris, the principal centre for French art pottery in the post-war era. He also served in the late 1950s on the jury of the Cannes Film Festival.

Paule Vézelay
1892-1984

Sculptor, designer, painter, printmaker, writer and collagist, born Clifton, Bristol as Marjorie Watson-Williams but changed her name in the 1920s whilst in Paris. Vézelay studied in Bristol; at the Slade and the London School of Art; and then lithography at Chelsea Polytechnic. She was part of the

London Group, 1922-32, but settled in Paris in 1926, and was increasingly influenced by abstraction and the School of Paris. She knew Picasso, Kandinsky and Gris and was involved with Abstraction-Création and Groupe Espace. After the war she returned to England. David Whitehead Ltd used one of Vézelay's paintings from the 1953 'Painting into Textiles' exhibition at the ICA, London, to produce a furnishing fabric. Knoll commissioned a furnishing fabric design from her and from the mid 1950s to the early 1960s she designed a series of furnishing textiles for Heal's Fabrics. In the 1940s Ascher also produced dress yardage and a printed head square to her designs.

Andy Warhol
1928-1987
Artist, designer and film-maker, Warhol was born in Pennsylvania and studied Fine Arts at the Carnegie Institute of Technology, 1945-1949. He was a seminal figure in the American contemporary art world of the fifties and sixties, challenging the distinctions between fine art and popular culture. Warhol initially worked as a commercial artist designing advertisements and covers for fashion magazines such as *Harper's Bazaar*, *Glamour* and *Vogue*, as well as other specialist journals. He held his first one-man exhibition at the Hugo Gallery, New York, in 1952. Throughout the 1950s he received numerous graphic design awards including the prestigious 35th Annual Art Directors Club Award for outstanding achievement for his I Miller Shoes advertisement, 1956. He produced illustrations for Fleming Joffe, an upmarket leather goods manufacturer and illustrated advertisements for NBC Radio. In 1962 he set up a studio later known as the 'Factory', where he worked with large number of assistants helping to create multiple art works to his designs. Warhol produced over 75 films from the 1963 onwards. He designed textiles; greetings cards, for New Directions Publishing; gift-wrapping paper, posters and illustrated books. During 1949-87 he designed, or contributed drawings to, over 50 record covers, including jazz, classical, pop and rock genres: amongst them, the Rolling Stones; Count Basie; Liza Minnelli and Diana Ross. Warhol used a distinctive 'blotted line' technique to produce his early drawings and prints that can be seen in many of his textile and pattern designs. He is thought to have sold textile designs to Fuller Fabrics, circa 1957-58. A number of his textiles, printed by an unknown manufacturer, were given to Stephen Bruce, proprietor of Serendipity 3, to be made up into fashion items in the early 1960s. Nat Wager is credited with printing his 'Bright Butterflies' design used by Robert Sloan in 1960, for fashion garments, but it has not been possible to confirm the manufacturer of other Warhol textile designs in the Warhol archive and a number of other textiles that have been located, dating from the early 1960s.

Warner & Sons
The company was founded in 1892 by Benjamin Warner (1828-1908) as a silk weaving company in Braintree, Essex, and London, producing traditional patterns and avant-garde, commissioned designs. In 1932 Warners employed Alec Hunter (1899-1958) son of Edmund Hunter, founder of the St Edmundsbury Weavers, in their design studio as head of production, and he remained with the company until his death in 1958. During the 1940s and 1950s Warners' textile production was variable, but they took over Helios Ltd, which had been run by Marianne Straub, and with it the printing of such classics as 'Sutherland Rose' and the services of Straub. In 1957 they printed designs by Lynton Lamb, Edward Bawden, James Fitton and Milner Gray. Many of Warner's designs were used at the Festival of Britain, 1951. Their output became increasingly streamlined during the 1960s and from 1965 they introduced themed collections. Warners were particularly strong in 'Pop' prints, especially the 'Accent on Pattern', 'Programmed Pattern' and 'Stereoscopic' collections. Many of their designs were created by the in-house design team but they also commissioned designs from Bawden, and de Colbertaldo Dinzl regularly contributed designs during the 1960s. In 1970 Greef Fabrics Inc. purchased Warners. The name Warner Fabric plc was re-registered in 1987 and they were subsequently bought by Walker Greenbank plc.

David Whitehead Ltd
The company was founded in 1927 in Rawenstall, Lancashire. During the 1950s under the direction of the architect John Murray, and later Tom Mellor, another architect and painter, David Whitehead Ltd employed leading designers and artists of the day to bring good, avant-garde design to the man on the street. They launched their 'Contemporary' collection at the Festival of Britain in 1951, which consisted of largely low-cost, small-scale, roller-printed fabrics. They later developed a more exclusive range of hand screen-printed textiles for the more textural painterly designs. The company purchased a large number of paintings from the 'Painting into Textiles' exhibition in 1953, including work by Vézelay, Moore and Cawthra Mulock that were translated into successful designs. Whitehead also produced textiles by Eduardo Paolozzi, Jon Catleugh, John Piper, Mitzi Cunliffe, Lisa Grönwall, Maj Nilsson, Humphrey Spender, Robert Tierney, Merrick Hansell, Peter Kinley, William Scott, Sandra Blow and Louis Le Brocquy. The company continued its interest in textiles by artists holding an exhibition in 1969, called 'Living Art Fabric', which included designs by John Packenham, George Campbell, John Piper and Pádraig Macmiadhacháin. The firm was wound up following its takeover by Lonrho in 1970.

White Stag
This firm was a subsidiary of the Oregon-based Hirsch-Weis Manufacturing Company, originally a tent manufacturer that had branched out into ski wear in 1929 because the founder's son was a keen skier. There were few American ski wear manufacturers at this time and by the 1940s they had expanded their range to include all types of sportswear including sweatshirts, ski jackets and raincoats blouses, a hostess 'culottes' dress and fur jackets. Howard Gossage and Bob Freemen, two San Francisco-based ad men with ideas and experience about what sportswear would sell, approached the company in the early 1960s. Freeman and Gossage had secured the rights to certain Picasso's images for use on fabric through his Paris-based agent. White Stag engaged in the top-secret project to produce ski wear and leisurewear made from Picasso-designed fabrics including designs such as 'Figures', 'Triptych' and 'Musical Fawn'. Marketing was a key part of the success of the range and shop assistants were sent booklets educating them about Picasso's work so they could speak to clients in an informed way; the garments were advertised as the affordable way to own a piece by this master. Related to this project is a dress produced in 1963 by West House Juniors, a division of White Stag, using Picasso's 'Clown' design. In 1966 White Stag was purchased by Warner Brothers Company, which later became Warnaco Group. After Warnaco emerged from bankruptcy in 2003 the White Stag trademark was sold to Wal-Mart which now uses it as an in-store brand for their women's clothing.

Gerald Wilde
1905-1986
A painter and designer, born in London, Wilde attended Chelsea School of Art between 1926 and 1934 and, after serving in the Pioneer Corps during the Second World War, he held his first one-man show at the Hanover Gallery in 1948. In 1951 he designed the catalogue cover for 'Sixty Paintings for '51', an exhibition held at the Festival of Britain. Wilde participated in several Cotton Board exhibitions in the early 1940s and one of the designs he'd shown was subsequently produced as a textile by John Heathcoat & Co. Wilde was commissioned by Zika Ascher to design fashion fabrics; one of his designs printed on silk was used for a dress by Edward Molyneux, worn by Her Majesty the Queen when she was Princess Elizabeth, on the Royal Tour in 1947. Courtalds also produced some of his textile designs, one of which was used for a cover of the magazine *International Textiles* (later *The Ambassador*).